Cool Food for
Hot Chicks

1 3 5 7 9 10 8 6 4 2

Text copyright © Louise Holland and
Roberta Moore 2001

First published in the United Kingdom in 2001 by
Ebury Press · Random House · 20 Vauxhall Bridge Road
London · SW1V 2SA

Random House Australia (Pty) Limited
20 Alfred Street · Milsons Point · Sydney · New South
Wales 2061 · Australia

Random House New Zealand Limited
18 Poland Road · Glenfield · Auckland 10 · New Zealand

Random House South Africa (Pty) Limited
Endulini · 5a Jubilee Road · Parktown 2193 · South Africa

Random House Group Limited Reg. No. 954009

A CIP catalogue record for this book is available from the
British Library

ISBN: 0 09 188077 7

Designed by Lovelock & Co.
Photographs by Jason Moore
Styling by Anita Wright
Edited by Gillian Haslam

Printed and bound in Great Britain by
Butler and Tanner Limited

LOUISE HOLLAND &
ROBERTA MOORE

Cool Food for Hot Chicks

**Just for the girls,
a collection of over
100 luscious recipes**

EBURY
PRESS

CONTENTS

Acknowledgements

Our thanks to everyone who has been involved in getting *Cool Food for Hot Chicks* into shape – be they hot chicks or not! Once again, our special thanks to all at Ebury Press; in particular Fiona MacIntyre who we managed to convince again; to Denise Bates and Ciara Lunn for their patience and editorial genius and to Sarah Liesching, whose input is invaluable and very much appreciated.

To those hot chicks who were there at the beginning and came up with some great titles and ideas - Kate, Tracey, Sarah, Melanie and Sam. And thanks to Matt for his finesse with the barbeque tongs and feeding us all!

To Andrew Conrad who, as ever, came through with flying colours.

To Kate Winslet, Charlie Dimmock, Gwyneth Paltrow, Melanie Sykes, Ulrika Jonsson, Denise Lewis, Denise Van Outen and Nigella Lawson for kindly sharing their recipes with the hot chicks of today.

Dedications

Roberta
Here's to you Louise.

Louise
Here's to you Roberta.

FOREWORD

First there was *Larder Lads*, the indispensable cookery book for men which brilliantly did the job of sorting the men from the boys when it comes to getting down to it in the kitchen.

'But what about us girls?' was an all too familiar cry from the legions of hot chicks left out in the cold when it came to establishing their place at the stove. And so we started to think pink – *Larder Lads* needed a sister, a girl-friendly cookery book that would cover every occasion a hot chick might find herself in – well, almost.

We both thought it was a 'no-brainer' and, luckily for us, so did our publisher. Our girlfriends out there strutting their stuff gave us all the advice we needed and so now it's over to you – the hip, happening and hot, hot, hot chicks around – get into that kitchen and show those Larder Lads how to do it!

Roberta and Louise

Note
Cooking temperatures and times for the recipes in this book are for fan ovens. If you are using a conventional oven, increase the heat by 10°C/50°F. Alternatively, for recipes with long cooking times, cook the dish at the temperature given for an additional 10 minutes per hour.

hunting and gathering

Here's our 'What Not to Miss List'. All the equipment is discussed later on in this chapter.

Basic Utensils

- Knives (small paring knife, bread/carving knife, medium-sized knife, knife sharpener/steel)
- Food processor
- Hand blender
- Electric whisk (with three settings)
- Frying pans
- Casseroles/saucepans
- Roasting tins and baking trays
- Carbon steel wok
- Coffee grinder
- Pestle and mortar
- Wooden or plastic chopping board
- Glass Pyrex mixing bowls
- Measuring jug
- Measuring scales
- Measuring spoons
- Slotted wooden spoon
- Selection of wooden, metal and wire spoons (spiders)
- Small and medium ladles
- Tin opener
- Corkscrew
- Masher/ricer
- Flexible metal fish slice or turner
- Selection of spatulas
- Serrated palette knife
- Garlic crusher
- Hand (balloon) whisk
- Kitchen tongs
- Bowl scraper with rubber/plastic handle
- Grater
- Zester
- Pastry brush
- Ice cream scoop
- Small plastic mandolin
- Potato peeler
- Wooden pepper mill
- Colander and sieves
- Salad spinner
- Kitchen timer

Most women wouldn't dream of going out on the town without being fully prepared. Imagine getting ready for a first date without a hairdryer or, worse still, without the close proximity of a well-stocked make-up bag. Yet lots of people still try to get away with using poor-quality kitchen equipment when it comes to cooking and preparing food.

Using the right basic kitchen equipment is all-important and makes cooking so much easier. Although some kitchen equipment is expensive, it really is worth splashing out on something essential that you are going to use every day, isn't it? You can build up your 'batterie de cuisine' over a course of time, so don't worry if you can't tick off everything on our 'What Not To Miss List' just yet. Start with a good set of knives.

SAUCEPANS AND CASSEROLES

There are so many different varieties of saucepans now available to the consumer that it's easy to become confused and not know which to choose. Hopefully our list below will shed light on the process for you. It contains an outline of the types of saucepan that we think are best suited to all-round cooking and the sizes you should aim to have. Make sure you feel comfortable with your purchase – you want your saucepans to feel sturdy but not overly heavy or too light and flimsy.

Copper Saucepans These are the best you can buy, but they come with a rather hefty price tag. They're worth it though as they are an excellent conductor of heat and cool down rapidly. If you do decide to splash out on a set, make sure they are lined with stainless steel for easier maintenance and cleaning.

Enamelled Cast-ironware Heavy to hold and heavy on the pocket, cast-ironware is a good conductor of heat and is available in an array of bright colours. Not great as a saucepan but excellent as roasting trays and lidded casseroles when you need to cook at a constant temperature. Try not to put this type of cookware in the dishwasher – keep your rubber gloves to hand. The lidded buffet casserole made by Le Creuset is a perfect shape and size for anything.

Stainless Steel Saucepans After copper, stainless steel is the best conductor of heat. The bases of stainless steel pans are now made out of layers of steel, copper and aluminium for improved conductivity. If you choose these, make sure they have a good, strong metal handle. Although the handle will get hot (remember to use oven gloves), you can then start cooking on the hob and finish off in the oven. These saucepans are easy to clean and can go in the dishwasher.

Anodised Pans These pans have been chemically treated and there are many different types available. They conduct heat well and also provide a good-quality, non-stick surface, making them an excellent choice for frying or omelette pans. They are not recommended for dishwashers so be prepared to wash up. Highly recommended are Meyer-Anolon.

FRYING PANS

As mentioned above, go for an anodised version combined with a non-stick surface.

WOKS

Although carbon steel woks are the cheapest and the best conductors of heat, they need to be looked after – namely heating, proving and wiping after use. Non-stick woks are easier to maintain but have to be able to withstand the high temperatures required in stir-frying. Thypoon have an excellent cast-iron version.

ROASTING TINS AND BAKING TRAYS

Make sure you go for a strong, sturdy roasting tin or tray – you don't want something weak that will buckle. Cast iron is best but for a cheaper, adequate alternative, anodised aluminium is fine. Mermaid produces an excellent range.

WHISKING AND MIXING

Balloon Whisks These need to be springy and light; 26cm/10in in height is a good all-rounder.

Electric Hand Whisk These save on arm work! Any basic model, with two or three different speeds, will suffice.

Recommended Saucepan Sizes

Size	Diameter
Large	20cm/8in
Medium	18cm/7in
Small	16cm/6½in
Very small (optional)	14cm/5in
Sauté pan	24cm/9½in
with a depth of	5cm/2in
Lidded buffet	
casserole (cast-iron)	30cm/12in
(These are Le Creuset terms)	

Recommended Frying Pan Sizes

Size	Diameter
Very large	26cm/10in
Small	16cm/6½in

Recommended Roasting Tin/Baking Tray Sizes

37 x 26½ x 7cm (14½ x 10½ x 2¾in)
31 x 21½ x 5cm (12½ x 8½ x 2in)

Hand Blender An indispensable piece of modern kitchen equipment. Great for puréeing and blending in anything. It is worth spending a little extra to get a version with a small attachment for chopping herbs and spices.

Food Processor If you are only going to buy one piece of electrical equipment, make sure this is it. Food processors can blend, slice, purée, chop and mix all types of food. They also last for years and save on time and effort. Magimix is the best value for money. The smallest variety is the best.

Kitchen Spoons Wooden and metal spoons, plus a spider spoon (great for lifting anything out of a liquid), are all useful pieces of equipment.

SMOOTHING, TURNING AND FLIPPING: SLICES AND SPATULAS

Fish Slice or Turner These should be made out of flexible stainless steel and are particularly helpful for lifting and turning hot food.

Spatula Flexible metal/stainless steel, long, thin spatulas are very handy for turning or lifting and moving hot foods. Plastic bowl-scrapers or spatulas are essential for scraping and cleaning bowls.

Kitchen Tongs Stainless steel spring tongs are best for turning food. And men love them at a barbecue!

CUTTING, SCRAPING AND GRATING.

Knives These are probably the most important items in your kitchen equipment, as a good set of high-quality stainless steel knives will make your culinary life so much easier. Spend as much as you can on three or four basic knives and collect more as you go along. Start off with a bread/carving knife, a cook's knife (20cm/8in), a paring knife (10cm/4in) and a serrated palette knife, which has the advantage of being dual-use. Blunt knives are a real no-no, so keep your knives sharp with a sharpener or steel or else you will struggle with your cutting.

Chopping Boards Wooden boards are popular and do their job, although they do tend to crack and warp. Plastic polyethylene chopping boards don't look as good but are readily available and we prefer them. Try to use separate boards for raw meat, cooked meat and vegetables. Slip a folded damp cloth underneath to prevent the board slipping as you work.

Graters A medium-sized box stainless steel grater (four-sided) is the best.

Zester This is a very handy, inexpensive piece of equipment. It only takes moment to completely zest an entire fruit.

GRINDING AND MINCING

Pestle and Mortar Handy to have. The best types can be found in Thai or Chinese supermarkets.

Coffee Grinder This can be used not only for coffee but for spices too. Try not to use the same grinder for your spices as your coffee though!

Pepper Mill This is essential for freshly ground black pepper. Wooden is best (plastic is adequate but is more liable to break).

SIEVING, DRYING AND STRAINING

Colander Don't go for plastic – they are an accident waiting to happen because they melt. Stainless steel ones fitted with a stand are best (20cm/8in is a good size to have).

Sieves It is useful to have one plastic sieve as well as a metal one (plastic is good for cold sauces).

Salad Spinner No-one likes soggy salad leaves so buy a salad spinner from your supermarket!

Beat Botulism!
Here are ten tips for food safety and hygiene. Some of them might seem obvious but we've included them anyway.

- Take chilled and frozen food home quickly, then transfer to your fridge or freezer at once.
- Prepare and store raw and cooked food separately. Keep meat and fish at the bottom of the fridge.
- Get yourself a fridge thermometer and keep the coldest part of the fridge at 0–-5°C/0–0.41°F
- Check use-by dates and use food within the manufacturer's recommended period.
- Keep pets away from food – and dishes and worktops.
- Wash your hands thoroughly before preparing food, after using the bathroom or handling pets.
- Keep your kitchen clean. Wash worktops and utensils between handling food to be cooked and food to be served raw.
- Do not eat food containing uncooked eggs. The young, the elderly, pregnant women or anyone with immune-deficiency diseases in particular should avoid both raw and lightly cooked eggs. Although these days salmonella is very rare in eggs, always buy those stamped with the Lion Code of Practice. Keep eggs in the fridge – or below 20°C/68°F.
- Cook food well. Follow the instructions on the packet and if you reheat anything, make sure it's piping hot.
- Keep hot foods hot and cold food cold. Don't just leave them standing around.

For every girl's cupboard:
- Salt – Maldon is best
- Black, whole peppercorns
- Pink peppercorns – these have an unusual sweet flavour. And they're pink!
- Dried pasta – spaghetti, linguini, penne, tagliatelle
- Rice – Basmati, Carnaroli
- Flours – plain, corn, arrowroot
- Couscous
- Tinned tomatoes
- Tomato purée
- Sun-dried tomatoes in oil
- Nuts – pine-nuts, flaked almonds
- Pesto sauce (fine for emergencies, although fresh is better)
- Soy sauce, oyster sauce, fish sauce
- Black olives (buy they from a good deli and keep in your fridge)
- Harissa (keep in your fridge great to spice up anything you fancy)
- Parmesan cheese (block form and kept in your fridge)
- Oils – olive oil, extra virgin olive oil, sunflower
- Good-quality mayonnaise
- Vinegars – red wine, white wine, good balsamic
- Mustards – Dijon, wholegrain, English
- Dried mushrooms – morels, porcini
- Worcester sauce
- Good-quality chocolate – at least 65% cocoa solids
- Sugar – caster, dark muscovado
- Marigold vegetable granules

MEASURING

Scales Digital scales are particularly efficient as they can instantly incorporate any measuring bowl into the required weight. Being plastic, they are also easy to keep clean.

Measuring Jugs and Spoons Small and medium plastic jugs are best, as the glass variety can break. Measuring spoons often cut down on preparation time and effort.

OTHER PIECES OF EQUIPMENT

Tin Opener Prices vary enormously but the cheap ones do the same job as the expensive versions.

Corkscrew Utterly indispensable! Choose whichever you feel comfortable with but remember the cheap 'levered' ones can break easily.

Glass Pyrex Bowls Recommended sizes for these heatproof bowls are 28cm (11in), 18cm (7in) and 15cm (6in).

Ice Cream Scoop This makes serving ice cream so much easier as it retains heat when dipped in hot water.

Masher/Ricer A stainless steel masher/ricer is a good option. For a fine purée, go for a stainless steel ricer which looks like a large garlic press.

Potato Peeler Good Grips, a small kitchen equipment company, have come up with the ultimate version of the potato peeler. It's made of stainless steel and has a sturdy rubber grip. Two types are generally available; one is called a swivel and the other a 'Y' peeler.

Small Plastic Mandolin This is cheap, handy and produces perfectly uniform slices.

Ladles Medium and small sizes are recommended.

Kitchen Timer Essential when you have a few things on the go. Digital is best but don't let the battery run out!

THE WELL-STOCKED KITCHEN CUPBOARD

Good-quality, basic ingredients, such as oils, vinegars, herbs, spices and mustards, are an essential part of cooking good food and all can be easily stored. You can collect them over the course of time and they are readily available, so there is no excuse! You can get nearly everything you need in supermarkets but spending a little more on quality products makes all the difference. Never forget your seasoning – Maldon salt and freshly ground black pepper are essential.

HERBS AND SPICES

Herbs are a very important part of cooking. Growing your own is great as they'll always be on hand and fresh too. If not, find a good greengrocer who supplies fresh, good-sized bunches and keep them in the fridge.

Dried herbs are fine and do have their uses. Remember that the drying process concentrates their flavour so adapt the quantity you use in recipes – you'll need considerably less than fresh.

Spices are easy to keep as they can stay in your kitchen cupboard in an airtight container for six months to two years. Buy them loose and whole if you can, as spices which you can grind as needed are far superior to pre-ground. However, the small quantities you can buy in jars are good enough and cheap too.

Dried herbs for your kitchen cupboard:
- Oregano
- Thyme
- Rosemary
- Fennel seeds

To spice up your life, keep the following to hand:
- Hot curry paste
- Chilli powder
- Cumin seeds
- Saffron
- Coriander seeds
- Cardamom pods
- Paprika
- Tandoori paste
- Whole nutmeg

chapter two
working girl

For those working girls out there,

this chapter covers ideas for quick and easy midweek suppers and food for your lunchbox. Recipes such as Pilaff and Greek Salad can be prepared with minimal effort after a quick trip to the corner shop on the way home, and whatever you don't manage to eat can be your lunch the next day – ideal for those rainy days sitting behind your desk and even better for those sunny days when you can picnic in the park.

<table>
<tr><td>Serves 4
Preparation and Cooking Time:
10 minutes</td><td># Horiatiki</td></tr>
</table>

Possibly the simplest and most attractive salad from the Mediterranean. The combination of the olives, tomatoes and feta is quite unique. Make sure you use the freshest and best ingredients that you can find, and if possible actually from Greece.

Utensils Nothing apart from a knife and a large serving bowl

12 ripe flavoursome tomatoes 225g/8oz feta cheese, preferably Greek 1 red onion 12 kalamata black olives	**1** Cut the tomatoes into large chunks and the feta into medium chunks (roughly half the size of the tomatoes). Halve the onion and slice thinly. Throw all the ingredients into the large serving bowl along with the olives.
Juice of 1 lemon 5 tablespoons extra virgin olive oil Small bunch flat leaf parsley, roughly chopped Sea salt and freshly ground black pepper	**2** Drizzle over the lemon juice and olive oil. Throw in the parsley, season well and gently mix.
Pita bread	**3** Serve in its full, unadulterated glory with warm pita bread.

<table>
<tr><td>Serves 2–4
Preparation and Cooking Time:
20 minutes</td><td># Herb Bread</td></tr>
</table>

Utensils Mixing bowl, palette knife or teaspoon, foil

1 small baguette or ciabatta bread	**1** Pre-heat the oven to 200°C/400°F/Gas 6. Slice the bread on the diagonal without cutting all the way through and place it on a very large piece of foil.
2 tablespoons fresh thyme 2 tablespoons chives ½ clove garlic, crushed 50g/2oz butter, softened Sea salt and freshly ground black pepper	**2** Chop all the herbs and mix with the crushed garlic and softened butter. Season well and spread on the bread in between the incisions. Wrap well in the foil and bake in the oven for 15 minutes. Open the foil for the last 5 minutes of cooking so the bread becomes crisp. Serve while still warm.

WORKING GIRL | **19**

Lamb Koftas

Koftas originate in the Middle East, where each area has its own version using many different flavours. This is a basic recipe to which you can add pine nuts or half a teaspoon of harissa (see page 79) for a spicy Moroccan feel. The quantities given below will serve four as a starter. You could try the smaller versions for canapés or a barbecue.

Utensils Large mixing bowl, large frying pan, pestle and mortar or electric coffee grinder, 20 small wooden skewers

1 onion
450g/1lb minced lamb

1 Grate the onion and mix with the lamb.

1 teaspoon coriander seeds
1 teaspoon cumin seeds
1 teaspoon chilli powder

2 Using the pestle and mortar or electric grinder, blend the spices to a fine powder and add to the lamb along with chilli powder.

2 tablespoons flat leaf parsley
2 tablespoons pine nuts
1 teaspoon dried oregano

3 Chop the parsley and add to the bowl along with the pine nuts and oregano. Mix well, using your hands.

4 Take a small handful of the mixture, push onto a small wooden skewer and mould into a sausage shape measuring roughly 7.5cm/3in in length. This amount should make 20 koftas.

A couple of tablespoons of
olive oil

5 Heat a little oil in a frying pan and fry the small kebabs for 3–4 minutes on each side.

½ cucumber, grated
142ml/5fl oz natural yoghurt
2 tablespoons mint, finely
chopped
Sea salt and freshly ground
black pepper

6 Mix the yoghurt with the cucumber and the finely chopped mint. Season and serve with the hot koftas.

Spiced Lentils with Minted Yoghurt and Flat Bread

Serves 4

Preparation and Cooking Time:
45 minutes

In the Middle East all dishes are served with some sort of flat bread, hence the pita bread for this one. It makes the recipe a little more substantial – a very quick and easy supper using store cupboard ingredients.

Utensils Large saucepan, electric coffee grinder or pestle and mortar

2 tablespoons vegetable oil
1 onion
1 teaspoon coriander seeds
1 teaspoon cumin seeds
½ teaspoon allspice

1 Heat the oil in the pan, finely chop the onion and fry gently for a few minutes until golden. Using a coffee grinder or pestle and mortar, grind the spices then add them to the pan. Heat them through to release the full flavour.

400g/14oz Puy lentils
800ml/1¼ pints vegetable stock

2 Add the lentils and cold stock, stir and bring to a gentle simmer. Cook gently, uncovered, for 20–25 minutes on a low heat. When cooked, the stock will have evaporated leaving the lentils loosely covered in a spiced stock. They will be just cooked but will retain their shape.

200ml/7fl oz natural yoghurt
¼ lemon, juiced
Small bunch fresh mint, finely chopped
Sea salt and freshly ground black pepper

3 Mix together all the ingredients for the flavoured yoghurt and season.

Pita bread

4 Season the lentils and serve warm with warmed pita bread and a good spoonful of the minted yoghurt.

Griddled Salmon with Tabbouleh

Salmon is one of the cheapest types of protein and is now widely available. Try to buy it as fresh as possible and, budget permitting, go for wild salmon, which is at its best from February to August.

Utensils Griddle pan or frying pan, large heatproof bowl

2 teacups bulgar (cracked instant) wheat

1 Put the wheat into a large bowl, cover with boiling water and leave for 30 minutes.

2–3 spring onions
4 medium plum or vine tomatoes, skin on
4 tablespoons olive oil
Juice of 1 lemon

2 Meanwhile, slice the spring onions into 5mm/1⁄4in slices and the tomatoes into 1cm/1⁄2in cubes. Drain the water from the wheat and place in a large bowl together with the tomatoes, spring onions, olive oil and lemon juice.

Large bunch mint
Large bunch flat leaf parsley
Sea salt and freshly ground black pepper

3 Roughly chop the mint and parsley and add both to the tabbouleh (cracked wheat) with plenty of seasoning; mix well. Cover and leave to stand for about 30 minutes to allow the flavours to infuse, but don't leave it too long as it will become soggy.

4 x 150g/5oz pieces salmon fillet

4 Over a high heat, heat up the frying pan or griddle pan, season the fish and cook for 4 minutes each side (take care it doesn't break when turning it over). When ready, the fish should still be moist in the middle.

Aged balsamic vinegar, for drizzling
Olive oil, for drizzling

5 Place a spoonful of the tabbouleh on a plate and place the salmon on top. Season and then drizzle with a little balsamic vinegar and olive oil.

Singapore Vegetable Noodles

The ready-cooked, straight-to-the-pan noodles now widely available are superior and far easier to use than the packet and dried varieties. Add curry paste to give them an extra spicy flavour. These are great for lunchbox food, cold or hot.

Utensils Wok

1 green chilli
1 red pepper
2 cloves garlic
5 cm/2in piece fresh ginger
125g/4½oz Shiitake mushrooms
5 spring onions

1 Remove the seeds from the chilli and finely chop. Cut the pepper in half, remove the seeds and slice thinly lengthways. Crush the garlic and grate the ginger. Thinly slice the mushrooms and spring onions.

2 tablespoons sesame oil
1 teaspoon curry powder

2 Heat the wok, add the sesame oil and, when smoking, add the chilli, garlic and ginger; stir well. Add the pepper, mushrooms, spring onions and curry powder. Keep on a high heat and stir-fry.

115g/4¼oz beansprouts
300g/11oz fresh cooked egg noodles
1 tablespoon fish sauce
3 tablespoons Mirin (sweet rice wine)
Small bunch coriander, chopped
1 tablespoon oyster sauce
Sea salt and freshly ground black pepper

3 After a few minutes, add the beansprouts and noodles, using your hands to gently break up the noodles. While stirring, add the fish sauce, Mirin, coriander and oyster sauce. Stir well again for a couple of minutes and serve when the mushrooms and peppers have just wilted. Season to taste.

Curried Chicken Salad

This is great for using up any leftover chicken or turkey. It is very important to ensure that you cook out your curry paste as it mustn't be used 'raw'.

Utensils Small baking tray, medium saucepan, medium glass bowl

4 corn-fed chicken breasts
Sea salt and freshly ground
black pepper
300ml/½ pint hot vegetable
stock

1 Pre-heat the oven to 190°C/375°F/Gas 5. Place the chicken in a small high-sided baking tray, season and pour over the hot stock. Cover with foil and place in the oven to poach for 15 minutes. Remove from the oven and leave to cool in the liquid. Keep chilled in the fridge until needed, (you can do this the day before) or alternatively you could use leftover cooked chicken.

Olive oil
1 onion, chopped
½ clove garlic, chopped

2 Heat the oil in the saucepan, cook the onion until soft and add the garlic.

1 heaped dessertspoon hot
curry paste, e.g. Madras
1 teaspoon tomato purée
1 tablespoon apricot jam
2 slices lemon

3 Stir in the curry paste, tomato purée, apricot jam and 150ml/5fl oz water. As it starts to simmer, add the lemon slices. Leave on a medium heat for 5 minutes for the flavours to infuse.

5 heaped tablespoons good-
quality mayonnaise

4 Strain the curry sauce straight into a bowl and, when cool, add the mayonnaise and season well.

100g/4oz slivered almonds
225g/8oz green grapes,
seedless or large ones cut in
half and de-seeded
100g/4oz dried apricots, cut
into thin strips

5 Grill the almonds by placing them under a high grill. Keep a close eye on them to make sure they don't burn. Prepare the apricots and grapes. Chop the chicken into eight pieces and add everything to the mayonnaise. Stir and season well.

Smoked Haddock Chowder

Using ready-made fish stock and fresh smoked haddock adds flavour to this substantial soup. It is best when you can get new season Jersey Royal potatoes during May.

Utensils Medium shallow pan, large saucepan

280ml/9fl oz tub fresh fish stock
225g/8oz smoked haddock

1 Pour the stock into a measuring jug and top up with water to make 1 litre/1¾ pints. Heat in the shallow pan and add the haddock, skin-side up. When it starts to simmer, time and cook for 10–15 minutes. Remove the fish from the stock, place on a plate and leave to cool. Once cool, break it into flakes and remove any skin or bones. Keep the stock for step 3.

Large knob butter
1 onion, sliced

2 Heat the saucepan, add the butter and fry the onion until soft.

About 8 new potatoes
2 fresh corn cobs
100ml/4fl oz white wine

3 Wash the potatoes and slice thinly. Cut the kernels from the corn on the cob. Add these and the wine to the saucepan with the onions. Pour in the strained stock and bring to the boil. Simmer for about 10 minutes or until the potato is cooked.

2 tablespoons chopped parsley
2 tablespoons chopped chives
3 tablespoons cream
Sea salt and freshly ground black pepper

4 Just before serving, add the flaked fish, herbs and then the cream. Taste and season.

Penne Pasta with Chicken and Red Peppers

Serves 4
Preparation and Cooking Time:
40–45 minutes

This is a very simple supper dish which can be easily re-heated the next day for lunch. You can add as much crème fraîche as your conscience will allow – you could also stir in some Mozzarella just before serving if you wish.

Utensils Large saucepan, casserole dish

1 large onion, finely chopped
2 tablespoons olive oil
2 cloves garlic, crushed
Sea salt and freshly ground black pepper

1 Gently fry the onions in the olive oil in the casserole dish over a low to medium heat. After a few minutes add the garlic and season well.

4–5 good-size chicken breasts, skinned, cut in half and sliced thinly on the diagonal

2 Once the onions are transparent and soft, add the chicken and gently fry for about 10 minutes over a medium heat until the chicken is cooked through.

400–450g/14–16oz penne pasta
800g/1¾lb tin peeled plum tomatoes
1 bay leaf
1 tablespoon dried oregano
1 teaspoon dried thyme
2 tablespoons fresh basil, torn
2 teaspoons tomato purée
50ml/2fl oz white wine

3 Bring a large pan of salted water to the boil and start to cook the penne over a medium heat until 'al dente' – this should take about 7-9 minutes.

Once the chicken is cooked through, add the tomatoes, bay leaf, oregano, thyme, basil, tomato purée and wine to the casserole dish and leave for a couple of minutes to allow the flavours to develop.

1 green pepper, de-seeded and sliced into small strips
2 red peppers, de-seeded and sliced into small strips

4 Add the peppers and season as required. Cover and leave to simmer gently for about 5–7 minutes.

3–4 generous tablespoons crème fraîche
Parmesan cheese, to serve

5 Drain the pasta and add to the casserole dish. Stir in the crème fraîche and check the seasoning. Sprinkle freshly grated Parmesan cheese over the pasta and serve with a crisp green salad and garlic bread.

Escalopes of Chicken with a Spiced Rub and Summer Raita

Serves 4

Preparation and Cooking Time:
20 minutes

Utensils Food processor, coffee grinder or pestle and mortar, large frying pan

Small bunch chives
Small bunch dill
Small bunch parsley
Small bunch mint
200ml/7fl oz Greek yoghurt
1 tablespoon olive oil
¼ lemon
Sea salt and freshly ground black pepper

1   To make the raita, throw all the herbs into a food processor and roughly chop. Add the rest of the ingredients and blend; season well. Cover and chill until ready to eat.

4 chicken breasts
4 teaspoons cumin seeds
4 teaspoons coriander seeds

2   To prepare the chicken, place a breast in a medium plastic bag and, using a rolling pin, beat the breast evenly until it becomes a thin, even escalope measuring roughly 15cm/6in long and 5mm/¼in thick. Do the same to all the breasts, then cover and chill until ready to use. Using the coffee blender or pestle and mortar, grind the spices and spread evenly on a large plate. Season with salt and pepper.

4 tablespoons olive oil

3   Heat the oil in a large frying pan, dip and press each escalope into the ground 'rub' to lightly cover one side. Fry gently for a few minutes on each side until golden brown and firm. Cook in stages and keep warm in the oven if your frying pan is not large enough to accommodate all the escalopes at once. Serve with a spoonful of the raita, a crisp green salad and new potatoes with chives.

Serves 4

Preparation and Cooking Time:

20 minutes

Suleiman's Pilaff

This is great for using up roast lamb. It is a version of an old Elizabeth David recipe.

Utensils 1 medium saucepan with lid

4 tablespoons oil
1 onion, chopped
1 clove garlic, chopped

1 Pre-heat the oven 190°C/375°F/Gas 5. Heat the oil in the saucepan and add the chopped onion. Cook on a medium heat until soft, then add the garlic.

200g/7oz rice
900ml/1½ pints vegetable stock

2 Throw in the rice and stir to coat with the oil. Add all the stock and bring back to the boil.

1 small handful raisins
1 small handful sultanas
1 teacup cooked lamb, diced
200g/7oz pine nuts, toasted

3 Throw in the raisins, sultanas and lamb, cover and cook in the oven for 15 minutes. Place the pine nuts on a small baking tray to toast in the oven until golden.

3 tomatoes

4 Meanwhile, halve the tomatoes, remove the seeds and chop into 1cm/½in cubes.

Sea salt and freshly ground black pepper

5 When the rice is cooked, add the chopped tomatoes and toasted pine nuts, season and stir quickly and put the lid back on. Leave for 5 minutes, then serve.

Tagliatelle with Artichokes and Sundried Tomatoes

Serves 2
Preparation and Cooking Time:
20 minutes

Utensils 1 large serving bowl, large saucepan

5 anchovy fillets
2 teaspoons capers, rinsed and dried
2 tablespoons grainy mustard
12 black olives
2 tablespoons fresh basil, torn
Small bunch flat leaf parsley, roughly chopped

1 Chop the anchovy fillets and place in a large serving bowl along with the capers, mustard, pitted olives, basil and parsley.

4 sundried tomatoes
4 halves jarred artichokes in oil, drained

2 Slice the sundried tomatoes and the artichokes and add to the rest of the ingredients in the large serving bowl.

100g/4oz dried tagliatelle
3 tablespoons olive oil
Sea salt and freshly ground black pepper

3 Bring a large pan of salted water to the boil. Throw in the pasta and cook for 3–4 minutes. Drain and gently toss with the other ingredients and the oil in the serving bowl. Season and serve with a rocket salad.

Denise Lewis' Bagged-up Jamaican Tilapia

Serves 2

Preparation and Cooking Time:

40 minutes

This is Denise's favourite simple and healthy fish supper dish. Tilapia is a freshwater fish widely available in most supermarkets.

Utensils Foil, medium baking tray

450g/1lb tilapia
Sea salt and freshly ground black pepper

1   Pre-heat the oven to 200°C/400°F/Gas 6. Wash the fish and place on a large piece of foil on a baking tray; season well.

8 cherry tomatoes, halved
½ bunch spring onions, finely sliced, including the green stems
250g/9oz asparagus tips

2   On top of the fish place the tomatoes, sliced spring onions and asparagus tips. Season again and loosely wrap, making sure the foil is secure at each end. Place in the oven for 20–25 minutes or until cooked.

3   Remove from the oven and carefully open the foil. Remove each fillet from the main bone and serve immediately with steamed vegetables and rice.

Duck Breasts with Lime and Honey

Serves 2

Preparation and Cooking Time:

15 minutes

Duck breasts can be the ideal solution for a 'special treat'. Magret ducks are the best if you can find them, if not go for organic. The lime is a perfect match to the duck's richness.

Utensils 1 medium frying pan, medium baking tray

2 medium duck breasts
Sea salt and freshly ground black pepper
2 shallots

1   Pre-heat the oven to 200°C/400°F/Gas 6. Heat the frying pan over a high heat. When the pan is good and hot, sear the breasts, skin side down first, for one minute each side. Move them onto the baking tray; season and cook in the oven for 10 minutes. Gently fry the shallots in the same pan until soft.

100ml/3½fl oz vegetable stock
¼ glass white wine
2 limes – 2 zested, 1 juiced
1 teaspoon honey

2   Meanwhile to make the sauce, add the stock and wine to the same pan and bring to the boil. When at a steady boil, add the lime zest and juice and honey and simmer for 3–4 minutes. The sauce will still be quite clear. Taste and season.

3   Serve with rice pilaff and creamed spinach. The breasts can be served either whole or diagonally sliced with the sauce drizzled over.

Gwyneth Paltrow's Marinated Grilled Swordfish

Serves 4
Preparation and Cooking Time
1 hour, plus 1 hour marinating:

Marinated, grilled swordfish with quesadillas filled with caramelised onions and different cheeses is a recipe Gwyneth makes when she's in the mood for a light dish that has a lot of flavour. This recipe is easy and really delicious, especially when served with the salsas. You can use other fish such as tuna or sea bass. The fish can be cooked under a hot grill or on a barbecue. If you wish, make the two salsas and the guacamole in advance and store, covered, in the fridge.

Utensils Large dish for marinating, food processor, heavy-based saucepan, frying pan

4 swordfish steaks
5–6 limes
Olive oil
Small bunch coriander
Sea salt and freshly ground black pepper

1 Wash the fish well with cold water. Place the steaks in a dish large enough to contain them without touching one another. Halve the limes and squeeze the juice all over the fish. Splash olive oil over the fish as well (there should be less oil than lime juice). Coarsely chop the coriander and add to the dish. Season with salt and pepper. Cover with cling film and refrigerate for one hour. Halfway through the marinating time, turn the fish over. (If you are pressed for time, you can marinate for just 15 minutes a side, but it's better to leave it longer.)

1 fresh, fragrant mango
Equal weight of ripe yellow tomatoes
Handful of coriander or basil
1 small onion
Sea salt and freshly ground black pepper

2 While the fish is marinating, make the mango and yellow tomato salsa to serve on top of the fish. Roughly chop a the mango and yellow tomatoes. Chop the coriander or basil and the onion. Mix in a bowl and season with salt and pepper to taste.

About 6 ripe red tomatoes
1 small onion
1 clove garlic
1 small chilli (optional)
Small bunch coriander

3 To make the red salsa for the quesadillas, roughly chop the red tomatoes and onion. Chop the garlic and chilli (if using). Mix together in a bowl with lots of roughly chopped coriander.

2 ripe avocados
Squeeze of lemon juice
Sea salt

4 To make the guacamole, simply process really ripe, tasty avocados with a little lemon juice and sea salt. Pour into a serving bowl.

2 large onions	**5** While the fish is still marinating, thinly slice the onions. Warm some olive oil in a heavy-based saucepan, add the onions and cook over a medium heat until they are caramelised.
Olive oil	

Olive oil	**6** To make the quesadillas, heat some olive oil in a frying pan. Take the soft corn tortillas and divide the fried onions between them. Add the goat's cheese to one tortilla and the other cheese to the second tortilla. Lightly fry until the cheese melts and the tortillas are golden in colour. When the quesadillas are cooked, cut them into quarters (so each person can be served with the different cheeses).
4 soft corn tortillas	
1 medium goat's cheese, crumbled	
Handful of grated Gruyère or Cheddar, or handful of crumbled mild blue cheese	

7 Pre-heat the grill (or barbecue). Remove the swordfish steaks from the marinade and grill for 5–6 minutes on each side.

8 Serve the fish with the mango salsa on top, the red salsa on the quesadillas and the guacamole on the side. Accompany with grilled corn-on-the-cob or a crisp green salad with roasted peppers and grilled slices of red onion dressed with an aged balsamic vinaigrette.

Serves 4

Preparation and Cooking Time:
35 minutes

Haloumi with Beet Relish

You can use either raw or cooked beets for this recipe. Beets are cooked simply by simmering them in plenty of salted water for about 20 minutes until soft.

Utensils Medium non-stick frying pan

2 medium beetroot, raw or cooked and vacuum-packed

1 If using raw beets, cook them as specified above. Cut the cooked beets first into thin slices and then into thin strips (about the size of matchsticks).

1 red onion
4 tablespoons balsamic vinegar
1 tablespoon aged red wine vinegar
1 tablespoon capers, rinsed and dried
Sea salt and freshly ground black pepper

2 Chop the onion finely, tip into a bowl and add the rest of the ingredients; season and stir well.

2 x 250g/9oz haloumi cheese
1 tablespoon extra virgin olive oil

3 Cut the haloumi into 5mm/¼in slices and heat the oil in the frying pan. Once the oil is hot, lightly fry the cheese in batches until light brown. Remove and keep warm in the oven on the serving dish.

4 When ready, check the relish for seasoning and then pour over half the cheese. Eat immediately.

Serves 4

**Preparation and Cooking Time:
5 minutes**

Green Salad

We are now almost overwhelmed with bags of ready-made salads in the supermarkets, but we have yet to find a good one. This salad combination utilises good quality bagged rocket, watercress and spinach. With the addition of some fresh herbs, you can easily make a far superior salad than anything you will find ready-made. Taking the trouble to prepare your own dressing makes all the difference.

90g/3½oz bag baby spinach
90g/3½oz bag watercress
Small bunch fresh basil or
fresh mint

1 Throw the spinach into a salad bowl. If using a bag of watercress, pick off all the long stalks. Pick the leaves of basil or mint and add according to taste.

½ cucumber
A small handful fresh chives,
chopped

2 Peel the cucumber and cut away the four sides from the seeds, then cut the 'edges' into strips and then into 5mm/¼in squares. Throw in with the leaves. Add the chopped chives.

1 teaspoon Dijon mustard
3 tablespoons sunflower oil
½ tablespoon white or red wine
vinegar
2 tablespoons water
Sea salt and freshly ground
black pepper

3 Mix all the ingredients for the dressing together, either in a bowl or a lidded jar which you can shake.

4 Season the salad and mix gently; drizzle with just enough dressing to coat the leaves lightly. Using your hands, mix and serve straightaway as this will not sit well.

Top Tips Watercress is at its best by far from September through to November. Try to buy the large-leaf watercress sold in big bunches.

Make extra dressing and keep covered in the fridge. Cover the leaves with a piece of damp kitchen paper until ready to use.

chapter three
nibbles

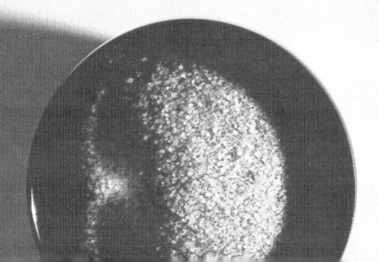

It's always handy to have a few nibble-y recipes

in your repertoire. Nibbles can be served instead of a starter, handed around at drinks parties or picked at while you and the girls are getting ready for a night out. Most of the nibbles we've included here can be made in advance and many have the added bonus of being light, so they won't give you a bloated tummy if you're planning on partying in your little black dress. And another thing – nibbles are perfect late-night munchie material!

The Classic Tomato Bruschetta

Serves 4
Preparation and Cooking Time:
15 minutes

This classic is a very popular and easy snack. You can either serve tiny versions as a nibble or make a larger version as a starter, served with rocket or black olives.

Utensils Griddle pan or toaster

16 good-quality ripe tomatoes
1 garlic clove, peeled and chopped
Large pinch of fresh or dried thyme or rosemary
Sea salt and freshly ground black pepper
Extra virgin olive oil
Aged balsamic vinegar

1 Halve the tomatoes and remove the seeds. Chop into small 1cm/½in squares and place in a bowl with the garlic and herbs. Season well, mix and drizzle with the oil and vinegar. This can be done in advance and left to mature for a while.

4 large slices of ciabatta or any country-style bread
1 clove garlic, cut in half lengthways
Extra virgin olive oil

2 Slice the bread and toast or char-grill using a griddle pan. While still hot, rub the bread with the halved garlic clove and drizzle with a little olive oil. You could cut the slices into smaller pieces if you wish.

3 To serve, pile as much of the tomato mixture as you can on to each piece of bread.

Bang Bang Chicken Wraps

Soft tortillas, now readily available almost everywhere, are used here as a wrap. You can use different fillings, but we think this combination of satay sauce, spring onion and cucumber with smoked chicken is the best. Cooked chicken could also be used.

Utensils Saucepan and sharp knife

125g/4½oz peanut butter
2½ teaspoons sweet chilli sauce
2½ tablespoons sesame oil
3 tablespoons sunflower oil
Sea salt and freshly ground
black pepper

1 Make the satay sauce by melting all the ingredients in a pan on a low heat and seasoning. Leave to one side.

½ a medium cucumber
3 spring onions
175g/6oz smoked chicken

2 Peel the cucumber and cut into chunks 6cm/2½in long. Cut each side away, leaving the seeds as a square which can be discarded. Cut each side into long, thin matchsticks. Cut the green end from the spring onion, remove the roots, halve it and then slice as finely as you can into long matchsticks. Cut the chicken into the same shape but slightly thicker.

4 soft tortillas

3 Lay a tortilla flat on a board and spread over a thick layer of peanut sauce. Trim the tortilla into a square shape, then cut into four equal lengths.

4 Put a few strips of cucumber, onion and chicken at the bottom of each tortilla strip, season and roll up tightly. Don't worry if some of the green garnish sticks out.

5 Serve the wraps straight away or keep covered in an airtight container for a few hours until needed.

Makes 80
Preparation and Cooking Time:
1 hour wrapping and chopping plus
a few minutes to fry

Spring Rolls

This recipe has been given to us by Roberta's children's nanny, Sheenly, who lived in Hong Kong for many years. Her special touch creates the lightest version of spring rolls that we have ever tasted, guaranteed to be devoured within minutes. Although quite time-consuming to prepare, they can be made in advance, frozen and cooked from frozen to order. Try looking in a Thai or Chinese supermarket for a range of chilli dipping sauces – they are normally far cheaper and keep well in your store cupboard.

Utensils Mixing Bowl, grater and saucepan

500g/1lb 1½oz fresh minced turkey, chicken, beef or pork
½ teaspoon salt
½ teaspoon pepper
2 tablespoons Hoisin sauce
1 carrot and/or 125g/4½oz water chestnuts, finely grated

1 Mix all the ingredients together in a bowl.

80 spring roll wrappers

2 Place about half a teaspoon of the filling in the corner of a spring roll wrapper. Roll up, folding in the corners as you go along. If the paper is too dry, it can be sealed at the edge using a little cornflour mixed with hot water to make a paste.

The spring rolls can now be frozen in a sealed container and cooked as necessary.

Vegetable oil
Sweet chilli dipping sauce or chilli jam (see page 55)

3 Fry a few at a time in piping hot vegetable oil until each roll is brown. Serve hot or cold with sweet chilli dipping sauce or chilli jam.

Top Tip You can also try making these with a vegetable stir-fry filling – try a combination of beansprouts, finely sliced cabbage, peppers, mushrooms and carrots. First fry the vegetables with a good amount of seasoning and a little chicken stock, and then go on to make your rolls.

Tapenade

This delicious traditional dip from Provence can be kept in the fridge for 8-10 days. It is a very useful spread as it's great on toast with any leftovers as a snack, spread in a roast beef sandwich or with grilled meat or fish.

Utensils Food processor

125g/4½ oz good-quality black olives

1 dessertspoon capers
2 dessertspoons olive oil
1 clove garlic
Juice of half a lemon

1 Remove the stones from the olives – you can use a cherry pitter but, as the olives will be blended, it is just as easy to use your hands.

2 Blend to a rough purée in the food processor or chop with the rest of the ingredients. Season well.

3 To serve, spread onto anything – toast is good.

Hummus

Traditionally hummus is a purée of chickpeas, served as a salad. However, in our version the addition of tahini (sesame paste) gives it a distinctive flavour, and you can use tinned chickpeas.

Utensils Food processor

400g/14oz tin of chickpeas
1 garlic clove
Sea salt and freshly ground black pepper

1 Drain the chickpeas and throw into the food processor along with the garlic and seasoning. Blend to a fine purée.

4 tablespoons tahini paste
A good squeeze of lemon juice

2 Add the tahini and blend again; give it a squeeze of lemon and taste. It's as simple as that!

Pita bread

3 Serve with warm pita bread.

Top Tip Hummus should be quite smooth so, if necessary, add a little water when blending.

Baba Ganoush

This is an authentic Middle Eastern dip which is great served at parties with any flat bread, such as pita. You can also serve it as part of an authentic mezze along with hummus (see page 42) and Creamed Aubergine Salad (see page 113).

Utensils Baking tray and food processor

3 aubergines **1** Pre-heat the oven to 190°C/375°C/Gas 5. Place the aubergines on a baking tray and bake for about 20 minutes until they soften. Cool and cut lengthways, then scrape out the inside flesh into the food processor.

2 cloves garlic
180ml/6fl oz tahini paste
½ teaspoon ground cumin
2 tablespoons parsley, chopped
Juice of 2 lemons
Sea salt and freshly ground
black pepper

2 Crush the garlic on a chopping board using the blade of a large knife, then chop it well and place in the food processor. Add the tahini paste and cumin and squeeze the lemon juice directly into the food processor. Blend to a purée and check the seasoning.

Pita bread **3** Serve with warm pita bread.

Guacamole

This ever popular dish is probably one of the easiest dips to make. It's already been in *Larder Lads* but we felt it's just too good not to include for the girls!

Utensils Food processor or fork

3 fresh green chillies
2 limes
3 ripe avocados
Large bunch fresh coriander
Sea salt and freshly ground
black pepper

1 De-seed the chillies and juice the limes. Using a food processor or a fork, blend all the ingredients together. There is no need for it to be a fine purée but if you are using a fork, chop the ingredients first. Season well and serve.

Avocado Salsa Croustades

Small crisp and light croustades can be found in most major supermarkets now and are great as a base for anything.

Utensils Sharp knife

1 avocado
¼ red onion, finely chopped
2 tablespoons chopped mint
Juice of 1 lime
Sea salt and freshly ground
black pepper
1 tablespoon crème fraîche
Olive oil

1 Cut the avocado in half and remove the stone. Peel away the skin, slice each half thinly and then cut into to tiny cubes. Place in a bowl with the onion, mint and lime juice and season. Gently stir together with the crème fraîche and a good drizzle of olive oil.

1 packet ready-made
croustades
Cayenne pepper

2 Using a teaspoon, spoon the avocado mixture into the croustades and top with a light sprinkling of cayenne pepper.

Top Tip Don't prepare the croustades too far in advance or they will become very soggy.

Potato Wedges

These simple chips make an easy but filling snack. They are pretty more-ish so be warned!

Utensils Large saucepan, large colander and very large baking tray

1.5 kg/3lb potatoes (Maris Piper or Red Desiree are the best)
Salt

1 Preheat the oven to 200°C/400°F/Gas 6. Cut the potatoes into half and each half into four. Place in a saucepan and cover with cold, salted water. Bring to the boil and simmer for 5 minutes. Drain.

3 tablespoons olive oil
Large knob of butter

2 Meanwhile, heat the oil and butter in the baking tray and place in the oven to heat well before adding the potatoes.

3 Sprinkle the salt over the cooked potatoes and throw onto the now hot baking tray. Roast for 40 minutes, turning occasionally.

Tomato ketchup or mayonnaise

4 To serve, drain on kitchen paper and serve with tomato ketchup or mayonnaise.

Quail's Eggs with Celery Salt

Possibly the easiest canapés in the world. Let your guests peel their own eggs and dip them in the celery salt.

Utensils 1 medium saucepan

1 pack of 12 quail's eggs   **1**   Bring a pan of water to the boil and place the eggs in it, bring back to a rolling boil and simmer for 3 minutes. Remove from the water and run cold water over the eggs for at least another 3 minutes.

Celery salt   **2**   Serve in a bowl or basket with a small bowl of celery salt for dipping. Let everyone peel their own eggs.

Top Tip If peeling beforehand, immerse the whole egg under cold water to make peeling easier.

Palmiers

These are classically a sweet petit fours, but this savoury version works just as well. Try using other fillings such as sundried tomatoes, pesto or blue cheese. If the rolls are made in advance, simply cut and bake the little slices as required.

Utensils Rolling pin, baking tray and cooling rack

1x 250g/9oz packet ready-made all-butter puff pastry
A little extra flour

1 Using a little flour, roll out the pastry to make it slightly thinner.

200g/7oz good-quality black olives
200g/7oz hard goat's cheese

2 Chop the olives finely and spread evenly over the pastry. Remove any hard rind from the cheese, cut into small cubes and sprinkle over the pastry.

3 Take the edge of the longer side of the pastry and fold over by 5mm/¼in, push down firmly. This will give you a good base to start to roll. Repeat the same on the other side. Begin to roll the two sides towards the middle, making sure that they are rolled evenly and meet in the centre. Wrap tightly in cling film and chill for 30 minutes or overnight.

4 On the day of eating, pre-heat the oven to 200°C/400°F/Gas 6. Cut thin slices of the rolled pastry approximately 5mm/¼in thick and lay flat on a baking tray, leaving a space between each one. Bake for 5 minutes or until golden brown. Leave to cool slightly before transferring to a cooling rack, then cut and bake the next batch. These can be kept in an airtight container but taste a lot better if cooked and eaten on the same day.

chapter four

entertaining adonis

'The way to a man's heart is through his stomach.'

We've all heard this saying before and most of us know that it's true. A man simply cannot resist good food, and having it prepared for him makes it (and you) all the more irresistible. Most men love a steak and this chapter gives three different steak recipes – the classic Rib Eye Steak with Chips, Steak with Béarnaise Sauce and the ever popular 70s' favourite, Peppered Steak. For those less red-blooded males, we've also included some fish recipes. One tip when entertaining at home – don't try to impress with complicated culinary masterpieces. Choose recipes that you're comfortable with and you won't go wrong.

Serves 2

Preparation and Cooking Time:
20 minutes

Spaghetti with Crab

Adding a little chilli to this rich, luxurious pasta dish gives it an interesting twist. The crab season is from April to August.

Utensils Large saucepan, small saucepan

250g/9oz spaghetti

1 Fill the large saucepan almost full of water and place over a high heat until it begins to boil. Measure the spaghetti and put to one side.

135g/4¾oz crab meat, brown or white or both (approximately ½ large dressed crab)

2 Weigh the crab meat and place in a small saucepan (any remaining crab can be used in a sandwich or salad the following day).

1 red chilli
Small bunch flat leaf parsley

3 Slice the chilli finely by cutting in half and using a teaspoon to remove the seeds. Then cut into full length thin strips and chop these again in the other direction to achieve small, even pieces. Add to the crab meat. Roughly chop the parsley and add three-quarters to the crab meat. Place the saucepan over a low heat.

Sea salt

4 By this time the water should be boiling for the pasta. Add a good spoonful of salt and the spaghetti. Cook on a high heat for 10 minutes for a good-quality pasta, or check the time on the packet instructions.

Extra virgin olive oil
½ large lemon
Freshly ground black pepper

5 Stir the crab mixture over the heat and squeeze over the lemon juice; add a good glug of oil, season and taste. The sauce should be fairly sloppy so, if necessary, add a little more oil.

6 Drain the pasta and pour back into the pan. Drizzle with a little olive oil and season well with salt and pepper. Pour over the warmed crab sauce and stir well to combine.

7 Pour immediately into two shallow bowls, drizzle with a little extra oil and sprinkle with the remaining parsley.

Scallop and Bacon Brochette

What could be simpler and more delicious than an exquisitely fresh scallop partnered with a good smoky piece of bacon? Hand-dived scallops are a must as their flavour is far superior to that of the small trawled variety which are never as fresh and taste rather insipid. A good fishmonger is your best bet for quality as the supermarkets haven't got it quite right yet! Use dry, cured bacon for a fuller, more satisfying flavour. You can make these on cocktail skewers for canapés if you wish.

Utensils 2 metal or wooden skewers, large frying pan

6 pieces dry cured streaky bacon
12 hand-dived scallops
Sea salt and freshly ground black pepper

1 Lay the strips of bacon flat on a board and cut in half. Lay the scallops on the edge of each piece of bacon, season well and roll up securely. Push onto a skewer. Continue to roll all the scallops with the bacon until both skewers are complete.

Good knob of butter

2 Heat the butter in the pan. When hot add each brochette, leave for 2½ minutes and then turn over. When cooked, they should be a good caramel colour and quite firm. If they are large, leave them to cook for a little longer.

2 good squeezes lemon

3 When ready, squeeze over the lemon, add a little more seasoning and serve on a bed of rocket dressed with balsamic vinegar and extra virgin olive oil. A wedge of lemon can also be served on the side.

Top Tip Make sure the scallops are medium-sized, dry and smell 'freshly fishy' – don't settle for anything less.

Rib Eye Steak with Chips

Serves 2

Preparation and Cooking Time: 30–40 minutes

A perfect chip should be crisp on the outside and meltingly soft on the inside. By making your own chips you should be able to achieve this without a great deal of fuss. The blanched chips can be made in advance and finished off when needed – this is always worth the extra effort. It's probably better to cook chips for no more than two as they do need to be cooked in small batches.

When buying steak, it is worth spending a little extra to ensure you get a piece of meat which has been cared for right down the line – the flavour and texture should be outstanding. Try to buy directly from the farmer to ensure you get the best available quality.

Utensils Griddle pan or baking tray, electric fat fryer or large saucepan

900g/2lb Maris Piper, Desiree or King Edward potatoes
2 litres/3½ pints vegetable oil

1 Peel and cut the potatoes into chunky chips, about 1cm/½in thick, and leave to soak in water while the oil is heating. If using an electric fryer set the temperature to 160°C, or if you use a saucepan, heat the oil gently until a piece of bread browns after 2–3 minutes. For safety, always ensure that the fryer is never more than one-third full. Drain and dry the potatoes and cook for 4–5 minutes or until soft in the middle, but without any colour. Drain and leave to one side. Turn up the heat to 190°C – the oil will be ready when a piece of bread browns in 1 minute.

2 x 175g/6oz rib eye steaks
Sea salt and freshly ground black pepper

2 Turn on the grill or heat the griddle pan until good and hot. Meanwhile, season the steaks with salt and pepper – do this a few minutes in advance to allow them to bleed slightly and 'relax' before cooking. For rare steak, cook for 2 minutes on each side; for medium, 3 minutes on each side; for well done, 5 minutes on each side.

3 While the steak is cooking, re-fry the chips for a few minutes until golden brown. Drain and pour onto kitchen paper. Season with salt.

4 Serve the meat and chips on a warm plate with a fresh, crisp green salad with a good dressing. Other accompaniments can be tomato sauce, mayonnaise or a good-quality mustard.

Pan Fried Scallops with Chilli Jam

Serves 2
Preparation and Cooking Time:
10 minutes

These quantities are perfect for two starter dishes.

Utensils Non-stick frying pan, palette knife

2 small handfuls rocket
A little sesame oil
Sea salt and freshly ground
black pepper

1 Throw the washed rocket into a bowl, season, toss gently in the oil and then arrange on two plates.

6 fresh hand-dived scallops

2 Lightly oil and season the scallops. Heat the pan and, when good and hot, place the scallops, with coral still attached, flat onto the base of the pan and leave to fry for 2½ minutes. Using a palette knife, turn over each scallop and cook for a further 2½ minutes until each side is a golden, caramel brown colour and quite firm.

2 tablespoons crème fraîche
2 tablespoons chilli jam (see
page 55)

3 When cooked, sit the scallops on the bed of rocket, topped with a spoonful of crème fraîche and a good drizzle of chilli jam. Serve immediately.

Top Tip Try to use only hand-dived scallops (see page 52).

Chilli Jam

This recipe is one of our favourites and has been adapted from Peter Gordon's book *The Sugar Club*. The jam only takes a little organisation to make and then keeps in a jar in the fridge. It perfectly complements the scallops but can be added to anything to spice it up – try it with a plain piece of fish or meat or anything you fancy.

Utensils Food processor, medium saucepan

5 cloves garlic
4 red chillies, green stems removed
3 x 2cm/¾in pieces fresh ginger
8 lime leaves
3 sticks lemongrass
1 teacup fresh ginger

1 Throw the garlic, chillies (seeds and all), lime leaves, lemongrass and ginger into the food processor and blend to a coarse purée.

300g/11oz caster sugar
4 tablespoons water

2 Stir the sugar and water together in a saucepan and keep on a low heat until dissolved. Turn up the heat and boil for 5-10 minutes until it turns a deep caramel colour – resist the temptation to stir until it turns the desired colour.

100ml/3½fl oz cider vinegar
50ml/2fl oz fish sauce
50ml/2fl oz Tamari

3 Stir in the purée, cider vinegar, fish sauce and Tamari and let this mixture simmer together for 1 minute.

4 Pour into jars and leave to cool before eating. Serve with Pan Fried Scallops (see page 54).

Tiger Prawns with Coriander Dressing

This recipe is quick and easy and tastes delicious. It's drawn from Gambas Pil Pil. Only use raw tiger prawns (heads on or frozen), don't settle for peeled. If you don't like to touch them, just move on to another recipe. These quantities are perfect for two starter dishes.

Utensils Large frying pan

200g/7oz raw tiger prawns

1 Peel the prawns by removing the shell, head and tail.

Small bunch fresh coriander
1 clove garlic

2 Roughly chop the coriander and garlic.

50ml/2fl oz olive oil
Sea salt and freshly ground
black pepper
Juice of 1 lime

3 Heat the oil in the frying pan. When smoking, add the prawns and stir fry for a couple of minutes. Add the garlic and seasoning. Continue to stir until the prawns turn a pale pink and are firm – at this stage they are semi-cooked. Stir in the chopped coriander and lime juice and heat through.

4 Serve in warmed shallow bowls with hot ciabatta bread to mop up the dressing.

Thai Mussels

The best time to buy mussels is in the autumn. They are cheap to buy and can now be purchased semi-cleaned. They don't take much preparation, particularly if you're only cooking for two and they look very impressive!

Utensils Large saucepan or buffet casserole

2kg/4½lb fresh mussels

1 Immerse the mussels in cold water and leave to soak. Meanwhile prepare the rest of the ingredients.

1 lemongrass stick
1 bunch spring onions
1 clove garlic
1cm/½in piece fresh ginger
1 red chilli
1 tablespoon sesame oil

2 Cut the lemongrass lengthways and then slice very finely along with the spring onions. Crush the garlic, grate the ginger (which doesn't need to be peeled). Remove the seeds from the chilli by cutting it in half and scraping out the seeds with a teaspoon, then slice thinly.

3 Back to the mussels. Clean and pull away any seaweedy bits from around the bottom. The most important thing when preparing mussels is to check if any are open. If they close when tapped you can keep them but if not discard them or you may run the risk of upsetting your guest! Once sorted through, keep the mussels covered with a damp cloth in a cool place until ready to use. The final cooking stage doesn't take long at all.

Sesame oil
2 limes zested, 1 juiced
200ml/7fl oz fresh fish stock
Small bunch fresh coriander
2 tablespoons fish sauce

4 Heat the pan, add a little sesame oil and lightly fry the onions and lemongrass on a medium heat. Add the ginger, chilli, garlic and lime zest and juice and leave to cook until soft. Pour in the stock. Half-fill the empty stock container with water, add to the pan and turn up the heat. Pour in the mussels and, when boiling, cover with a lid and simmer for 5 minutes.

Salt and freshly ground black peper

5 Using a slotted spoon, take out the cooked mussels, all of which should have opened to reveal their plump orange middles. Discard any that are closed. Keep warm in two large shallow bowls in a very low oven. Put the pan back onto the heat and bring the cooking liquid to a rolling boil. Leave to reduce for a couple of minutes until the sauce is slightly thicker. Add the chopped coriander and fish sauce. Season and divide the sauce between the two bowls and serve immediately with warm crusty bread.

Sirloin Steak with Sauce Béarnaise

This is bound to impress your man. It is a classic steak recipe, and the Béarnaise sauce is fresh and light and complements it perfectly.

Utensils Griddle pan or frying pan or baking tray, medium saucepan

2 x 175g/6oz sirloin steaks
Sea salt and freshly ground
black pepper

1 Season the steaks. If using a griddle pan, begin to heat it over a low heat. Meanwhile you can begin to prepare the sauce.

2 egg yolks
110g/4¼oz unsalted butter,
straight from the fridge,
cubed

2 Fill the saucepan a quarter full of water and bring to a fast boil. Place the egg yolks in a large bowl which will fit snugly over the saucepan without touching the water and turn the heat down to the lowest setting. Take a couple of tablespoons of hot water from the pan and add to the yolks. Whisk until light and foamy, then throw in a piece of butter and continue to whisk as it melts. If it looks too hot and the eggs change texture completely, remove the whole bowl from the heat, add more cold butter and continue whisking – the temperature of the butter will stabilise the sauce. If it becomes grainy and liquidy, add a couple of spoonfuls of hot water. As the butter is added, the sauce will become thick and glossy.

3 Start to cook your steak (if using a grill ensure it is good and hot). For rare steak, cook for 2 minutes on each side; for medium steak, cook for 3 minutes on each side; for well done steak, cook for 5 minutes on each side.

Juice of ½ a lemon
3 tablespoons fresh tarragon,
chopped

4 Stir the lemon juice and tarragon into the sauce. Taste, and season well. Serve on warm plates with a green salad.

Peppered Steak

Perhaps a little '70s', but always a winner with the blokes.

Utensils Pestle and mortar, large frying pan

1 tablespoon black peppercorns
2 x 200–250g/7–9oz rib eye
or sirloin steaks
Sea salt

1 Crush the peppercorns in a pestle and mortar or in a bowl using the base of a rolling pin – there should be some quite chunky pepper pieces left. Pour onto a plate. Lay one side of each steak onto the crushed peppercorns and then press down firmly. Salt well.

1 knob butter

2 Put the frying pan over a high heat and throw in the butter. Cook your steak according to taste and leave to rest while you finish preparing the sauce. For a rare steak, cook for 2 minutes on each side; for medium, cook for 3 minutes on each side; for well done, cook for 5 minutes on each side.

2 tablespoons brandy
3 tablespoons crème fraîche

3 Pour the brandy into the pan and ignite. Add the crème fraîche and a little salt. While this reduces, scrape the bottom of the pan to release all the meat flavours.

4 To serve, place the steaks onto warm plates and pour over the sauce. Serve with fried courgettes or spinach and potato wedges (see page 45).

Skate in Black Butter

This is a very simple and quick fish supper. The black butter perfectly enhances the delicate taste of the skate but be careful not to burn the butter – watch it carefully and take it off the heat as soon as it browns.

Utensils Roasting pan or wide pan, small saucepan

2 good-size skate wings
Sea salt and freshly ground black pepper
1 tablespoon white wine vinegar
1 bay leaf

1 Place the skate wings in a wide pan or roasting tin. Season and add the wine vinegar and bay leaf. Cover with cold water, bring slowly to the boil and simmer over a low heat for 10–15 minutes, but be sure not to overcook the fish.

75g/3oz butter
1 tablespoon white wine vinegar
Squeeze of lemon
2 tablespoons capers
2 tablespoons parsley, very finely chopped

2 Meanwhile, in a small saucepan slowly melt the butter over a low heat until it turns a rich brown. Remove immediately from the heat. Add the wine vinegar, a good squeeze of lemon, the capers, parsley and seasoning. Warm through gently over a low heat.

Lemon wedges

3 To serve, drain the cooked fish well. Discard the bay leaf and arrange the fish on a warm serving dish. Pour over the black butter and garnish with slices of lemon. This is particularly good served with new potatoes and wilted spinach.

Carbonnade of Beef

Although this recipe takes a while in the oven, it is well worth the wait. It's a rich and mellow traditional dish – the beef cut should be shin, which needs a long, slow cooking process to tenderise and improve the flavour. If you use beef shin from a butcher, ask him to remove the bone. However, if you're shopping in a supermarket, large pieces of braising steak will do. Freeze any leftovers for another day.

Utensils Large buffet casserole (30 x 6cm/12 x 2½in deep), tongs

1kg/2¼lb beef shin or braising steak
2 tablespoons beef dripping or olive oil

1 Pre-heat the oven to 150°C/300°F/Gas 2. Cut the meat into 5cm/2in cubes. Heat the oil in a large ovenproof casserole and when very hot add the meat a few pieces at a time. When they are a deep brown, turn using long tongs and brown the opposite side. Don't rush this or it will hinder the final flavour.

2 medium onions, sliced
1 tablespoon flour
1 clove garlic, crushed
425 ml/14½fl oz brown ale
425 ml/14½fl oz hot water
3 sprigs thyme
1 bay leaf
Pinch of grated nutmeg
Pinch sugar
1 tablespoon wine vinegar

2 Lower the heat, add the onions and seasoning and cook until brown. There should still be about ½ tablespoon of oil in the pan. Sprinkle over the flour, add the garlic, stir for a few seconds and return the meat to the pan. Add the hot water, beer, thyme, bay leaf, grated nutmeg, sugar and wine vinegar. Stir well to release any meat juices which may be stuck on the bottom of the pan. Season again, cover with the lid and cook gently in the oven for 2 hours. The meat will be beautifully tender and the sauce a rich thick mahogany.

1 tablespoon Dijon mustard
Chopped parsley to garnish
Sea salt and freshly ground black pepper

3 Stir in a spoonful of Dijon mustard and serve immediately. Sprinkle with some chopped parsley and serve with braised red cabbage and horseradish mash.

dinner party diva

Dinner parties should be all about having fun and enjoying yourself,

and not just for your lucky guests. Don't get sucked into feeling you have to go all out to impress, as these days it's really not necessary to prepare anything formal. Do as much preparation as you can in advance and you'll find entertaining so much easier and more enjoyable. We've given a wide variety of recipes here, ranging from Thai Fish Cakes with Chilli Jam to the 70s' favourite, Fondue – just perfect for a dinner party as the guests do the cooking themselves!

Red Thai Curry

This is not as hot and spicy as a green curry but uses the same principles.

Utensils Large casserole or ovenproof dish

700g/1lb 9oz chicken thighs, boned and skinned

1 Cut each chicken thigh in half.

1 lemongrass stick
4 lime leaves or zest and juice of 4 limes

2 Cut the lemongrass stick in half lengthways and slice finely. Remove the vein from the lime leaves and thinly slice.

400ml/14fl oz tin coconut milk
2 tablespoons red Thai curry paste
Sea salt and freshly ground black pepper

3 Pour the coconut milk into the casserole. Fill the empty tin with cold water and add to the pan; stir well. Remove half the liquid and put to one side for later. Bring the remaining liquid in the pan to the boil and simmer for 5 minutes to reduce. Add the curry paste and simmer for a further 5 minutes. Add the chicken, the remaining coconut milk, lemongrass and lime leaves; season well. Simmer, uncovered, for 40 minutes.

Large bunch fresh coriander
2 tablespoons fish sauce

4 When the chicken is cooked, you can add a little water to thin the sauce if required. Add the coriander and fish sauce and check for seasoning – remember the fish sauce is quite salty.

5 Serve with plenty of rice.

Charlie Dimmock's Shrimps in Sour Cream

Charlie enjoys having friends over for dinner. She loves seafood and this is a favourite recipe of hers as it is quick and easy to prepare. This starter can be prepared well in advance and then baked just before serving. If sour cream is not available, it can be made quite easily by adding the strained juice of half a large lemon to the same amount of double cream.

Small knob of butter
225g/8oz peeled shrimps
Freshly ground black pepper
150ml/5fl oz sour cream

1 Butter four small flameproof dishes and put about 2 tablespoons of shrimps into each. Season thoroughly with freshly ground black pepper and cover with sour cream.

1 handful fresh white breadcrumbs
50g/2oz unsalted butter

2 Sprinkle a thick layer of fine breadcrumbs over the cream and dot with knobs of butter. Bake in the centre of the oven for 10 minutes. Finish the shrimps under a hot grill for a minute or two or until the breadcrumbs are golden brown on top.

Parsley sprigs, to garnish

3 Garnish each dish with a sprig of parsley, and serve with chunks of warm wholemeal bread and butter.

Warm Smoked Salmon Filo Tartlets

Serves 4

Preparation and Cooking Time:
30 minutes

A very simple yet special starter for which the components can be organised in advance and easily put together at the last minute. Try these baskets with sautéed mushrooms mixed with chopped chives and a good squeeze of lemon, delicious with the hidden crème fraîche.

Utensils Small saucepan, pastry brush, four 12cm/5in tartlet tins, large baking tray

50g/2oz butter
8 sheets ready-made filo pastry (each sheet should measure approximately 31 x 17cm/ 12 x 6½in)

1 Pre-heat the oven to 200°C/400°F/Gas 6. Melt the butter in a saucepan. Place one filo sheet on a flat surface and brush evenly with butter. Fold neatly in half and place over a tartlet tin, pushing gently into the base to mould to the tin's shape. Brush this layer with butter. Repeat the process again, laying the second square at a 90 degree angle to the first. You should end up with four points in an upright position which can be trimmed neatly with scissors to just above the level of the tin edge. Brush again with butter. Repeat for the other three tins. Bake for 6–7 minutes until golden brown.

2 medium tomatoes
2 teaspoons fresh oregano

2 Skin the tomatoes by placing them in a bowl and covering them with boiling water. Leave them for 1 minute, then immerse in cold water and peel off the skin. Cut in half, remove the seeds and roughly chop. Roughly chop the oregano.

4 tablespoons crème fraîche
Sea salt and freshly ground black pepper
4 small slices smoked salmon, about 125g/4½oz

3 To assemble, remove the tartlets from the tins and place on a baking tray. Place a spoonful of crème fraîche on the base of each tartlet. Spoon the chopped tomato on top and sprinkle with oregano. Season well and then cover each with one slice of smoked salmon. Leave to chill in the fridge until needed.

Extra virgin olive oil
Small bunch fresh dill

4 Pre-heat the oven 200°C/400°F/Gas 6. Bake for 2 minutes just to heat through. Brush with a little olive oil and garnish with a sprig of dill. Serve immediately.

Thai Fish Cakes with Chilli Jam

These can be made in advance and then fried at the last minute. It is essential to serve them with a dipping sauce, hence the addition yet again of our favourite chilli jam.

Utensils Small baking tray, food processor, large mixing bowl, large non-stick frying pan

500g/1lb 1½oz cod fillet, skin removed
Sea salt and freshly ground black pepper

1 Heat the oven to 190°C/375°F/Gas 5. Cut the fish in half and place one half on a large piece of foil, season well and wrap tightly. Place on the baking tray and cook for 5 minutes. Leave to cool and reserve for later.

1 clove garlic
2cm/¾in piece fresh ginger
1 shallot, peeled

2 In a food processor, blend the garlic, ginger and shallot into a fine paste.

1 teaspoon chilli flakes
Small bunch fresh coriander
1 tablespoon fish sauce

3 Add the remaining raw fish and blend again. Add the chilli flakes, coriander and fish sauce and blend until smooth. Scrape into a large mixing bowl.

A little flour, a little oil and a knob of butter

4 Flake the cooled, cooked fish into large pieces and gently fold into the mixture. Season and divide into four. Shape into rounds roughly 8 x 2cm/3¼ x ¾in. Cover and chill in the fridge.

5 Lightly dust the cakes on both sides with flour and heat the oil and butter in the frying pan. When the butter is foaming, gently fry the fish cakes for 4 minutes on each side.

6 Serve with a drizzle of chilli jam (see page 55) or sweet chilli sauce, a green salad garnished with spring onion, cucumber and a sharp lemon dressing.

Root Vegetable Curry

A good winter, vegetarian recipe. Remove the coconut and it's a great recipe for a de-tox week.

Utensils Pestle and mortar or coffee grinder, buffet casserole or large saucepan

2 carrots
2 parsnips
½ swede
1 sweet potato
1 squash

1 Peel and cut the vegetables into 2cm/¾in squares. Be careful when peeling the squash – use a very sharp knife to peel away the thick skin and then remove the seeds.

1 onion
2 cloves garlic
2 tablespoon sunflower oil
2 tablespoons Madras curry paste
2 x 400g/14oz tins chopped tomatoes
Sea salt and freshly ground black pepper

2 Chop the onion finely and crush the garlic. Heat the oil in the pan and gently fry the onion and garlic. Add the curry paste and fry for a minute to release the flavours. Add the prepared vegetables, tomatoes and 100ml/3½fl oz water, season and stir well. Cover and cook on a medium to low heat for 20 minutes.

1 medium courgette
8 chestnut button mushrooms

3 Meanwhile, prepare the courgette by cutting into 1cm/½in slices and cut the mushrooms into quarters. When the 20 minutes has elapsed, add the courgettes and mushrooms to the pan and stir well. Cover and cook for a further 10 minutes.

4cm/1½in piece creamed coconut
Small bunch fresh coriander

4 To serve, cut the coconut into small pieces, chop the coriander and stir both into the curry. Serve with mango chutney and basmati rice.

Ulrika Jonsson's Marinated Roast Lamb

Marinating the lamb overnight in mint sauce is a clever and effortless way of bringing out the flavour of the meat – it is simply delicious, particularly when served with Ulrika's red wine and redcurrant gravy.

Utensils Roasting tin, whisk

1kg/2¼lb loin of lamb (off the bone)
200g/7oz mint sauce

1 Marinate the lamb overnight in the mint sauce.

500ml/17fl oz vegetable stock
½ clove garlic

2 Pre-heat the oven to 190°C/375°F/Gas 5. Place the lamb in the roasting tin and pour over the vegetable stock. Place the garlic next to the lamb and cover the roasting tin with foil. Place in the oven for about one hour if you like your meat pink; if not, cook for slightly longer.

1 tablespoon flour
¼ bottle red wine
4 tablespoons redcurrant jelly
Sea salt and freshly ground black pepper

3 Take the meat out of the roasting tin, leave to rest and then place the tin with the meat juice over a medium heat to make the gravy. Add the flour to the pan of meat juice and stir in the red wine. Add the redcurrant jelly and whisk until the jelly has dissolved. Taste and season as necessary.

Roast Cod with Salsa Verde

Salsa Verde is a classic Italian sauce. It can be kept in the fridge for up to a week. It's not only good with fish; try it with meat or even in sandwiches – it's great in a roast beef sandwich.

Utensils Food processor, large ovenproof non-stick pan

2 garlic cloves, peeled
Large bunch flat leaf parsley
Large bunch mint
2 tablespoons capers
1 tablespoon Dijon mustard
1 tablespoon wine vinegar

1 Pre-heat the oven to 200°C/400°F/Gas 6. Blend the garlic, parsley, mint, capers, mustard and wine vinegar in a food processor for a couple of minutes to make a fine paste.

150ml/5fl oz extra virgin olive oil
Sea salt and freshly ground black pepper

2 With the blade still turning, slowly add the oil, which will gradually give you a thickish sauce. Taste, season as necessary and put to one side.

4 x 175g/6oz pieces of cod fillet, skin on
A little olive oil
Knob of butter

3 Wipe the cod with kitchen paper so it is dry and then season. Heat the pan with the oil and, when hot, add the butter which should start to foam immediately. Place the cod fillets skin-side down into the pan. Place the pan in the oven for 10–15 minutes until the fish is just firm and the skin crispy.

4 Serve the fish on a hot plate skin-side up with a spoonful of the sauce over the top. Any spare sauce can be kept in the fridge in a jar and used with any other fish or meat.

Top Tip The pan should be large enough to take all the fish pieces and still leave a good gap around the edges, otherwise they will steam rather than roast. Use two pans if necessary.

Beef Fondue

This dish was popular in the 70s and is making a comeback. It is very simple to prepare and you and your guests will enjoy every minute of the cooking. Don't forget that a forfeit is imperative when you lose a piece of meat!

Utensils Fondue set, small saucepan

800g/1¾lb beef fillet or rib eye steak, cut into 1.5cm/¾in cubes

1 Divide the beef into four portions.

250ml/8fl oz jar ready-made hollandaise sauce
Small bunch fresh tarragon
1 shallot, finely chopped

2 Mix the hollandaise sauce in a small saucepan with the tarragon and shallot. Leave to warm through later.

4 tablespoons mayonnaise
1 tablespoon fresh pesto
Sea salt and freshly ground black pepper

3 Mix the mayonnaise with the pesto and season.

Creamed horseradish sauce
Chutney
Dijon or grainy mustard
Chilli jam (see page 55) or Thai dipping sauce (see page 75)

4 You will need about 4 tablespoons of each sauce that can be put into small dishes.

1 litre/1¾ pints sunflower or vegetable oil

5 Put the oil on the hob to heat and then transfer to the fondue pot on the stand above the little burner – it should be good and hot.

6 Serve with chips or potatoes on the table along with the meat and sauces – everyone helps themselves! Try stock instead of oil for a healthy alternative.

Lemon Roast Chicken

This adaptation, which made its first appearance in *Larder Lads*, of a Simon Hopkinson recipe is unlike any other roast chicken recipe. It's very simple and aside from the subtle flavour of lemon and garlic which perfectly enhances the chicken, it has the added bonus that its own delicious gravy is made during the roasting process. When roasting a chicken, it is better to spend that little bit extra on a superior bird. Try to go for corn-fed or free-range.

Utensils Large roasting tin, a small saucepan and sieve

50g/2oz unsalted butter, at room temperature
2 x 1.8kg/4¼lb free-range chickens

1 Pre-heat the oven to 200°C/400°F/Gas 6. Smear the butter over each chicken and place both, uncovered and breast-side down, in a large roasting tin.

Sea salt and freshly ground black pepper
2 lemons, halved and juiced
30g/1oz fresh thyme or tarragon
2 cloves garlic, peeled
275ml/9fl oz vegetable stock

2 Season well, then place the squeezed-out lemon halves inside the birds' cavities, along with the herbs and garlic. Pour over the vegetable stock.

3 Place the chickens, uncovered, in the oven. After 10 minutes, baste the bird with the stock and turn the oven down to 190°C/375°F/Gas 5. Roast for 50 minutes.

4 Check that the chicken is cooked by cutting through the leg – no blood should run from the thigh. Take the chicken out of the oven, remove the lemon, herbs and garlic from the cavity and add them to the roasting tin to help flavour the gravy. Let the cooked chicken rest in a warm place, covered in foil, for approximately 15 minutes.

1 teacup white wine

5 Add the wine and extra seasoning to the roasting tin, scraping the bottom of the pan as you stir over a medium heat. Push the lemons around the tin to extract all their remaining juices and leave to simmer gently for 5 minutes while the chicken is resting. Strain into a saucepan.

6 To serve, return the chicken to the roasting tin to carve it and pour any extra juices into the gravy saucepan. Reheat the gravy and serve separately.

Paella

Utensils Large flat-based pan (buffet casserole) or paella dish

2 tablespoons olive oil
4 chicken legs and 2 breasts,
free-range or corn-fed
Sea salt and freshly ground
black pepper

1 Heat the oil in the pan over a medium heat. Add the chicken pieces, season and fry gently for about 10–15 minutes until brown. Remove and set to one side.

1 large onion, chopped
1 red pepper, de-seeded and
cubed
1 green pepper, de-seeded and
cubed
2 large cloves garlic, crushed
3 plum tomatoes, quartered

2 Add the onion to the pan and fry for 4–5 minutes; then add the peppers and garlic, and fry for a further 4–5 minutes. Add the tomatoes and fry for 2–3 minutes until soft.

450g/1lb paella rice
A good large pinch of saffron

3 Stir in the rice, making sure it combines well with the vegetables. Add the saffron strands and combine.

1 litre/1¾ pints good-quality
chicken stock
150g/5oz frozen petit pois
175g/6oz chorizo sausage, cut
into 1cm/¾in slices

4 Pour in the stock and bring to a simmer. Add the peas and chorizo and season. Add the chicken, pushing it well into the rice. Cover and simmer for 25–30 minutes, shaking the pan occasionally.

18 uncooked mussels, cleaned
and de-bearded
300g/11oz raw tiger prawns,
unpeeled, heads and tails on

5 Scatter over the mussels and stir in the prawns, cook for a further 10–15 minutes until they have all opened (discard any that do not open) and the stock has been absorbed – the rice should be a little sticky.

1 tablespoon flat leaf parsley,
chopped
Lemon wedges

6 Serve in the paella dish straight to the table. Garnish with chopped parsley and with lemon wedges on the side.

Chicken and Lemongrass Brochettes with Thai Dipping Sauce

Serves 4
Preparation and Cooking Time:
25 minutes, plus 30 minutes
marinating

Utensils Medium glass bowl, small saucepan, large non-stick frying pan

6 tablespoons sesame oil
6 tablespoons fish sauce
2 teaspoons sugar
1 clove garlic, crushed
2 teaspoons dried chilli flakes
Large bunch fresh coriander,
roughly chopped

1 Mix all the marinade ingredients together in a bowl.

8 small corn-fed chicken breasts

2 Cut each chicken breast in half lengthways, then each half into 3 small cubes. Mix into the marinade, cover and refrigerate for at least 30 minutes.

160g/5¼oz sugar
300ml/10fl oz rice vinegar

3 Meanwhile, make the dipping sauce by stirring together the sugar and vinegar in a saucepan, gently bringing to the boil on a high heat. When a gentle boil is reached, turn the heat down and simmer until the liquid changes to a thickish syrup – this will take about 10 minutes. If the sauce is taken off the heat to settle this will give a better idea of thickness.

4 fresh red chillies,
1 clove garlic
2 tablespoons fresh coriander
1 teaspoon Sea salt

4 While this liquid is boiling, cut the chillies in half and remove the seeds with a teaspoon, then chop finely. Crush the garlic and roughly chop the coriander. Once the correct consistency is reached, stir these ingredients, with the salt, into the liquid and leave to cool. Pour into 4 small dishes or ramekins.

4 fresh sticks lemongrass

5 Cut each lemongrass stick in half lengthways and carefully push the chicken cubes onto each stick, which acts as your skewer. Divide the chicken evenly amongst the 8 sticks.

Salt and freshly ground black pepper

6 Heat the frying pan on a medium heat, then gently cook each brochette for 8–10 minutes each side, turning once and seasoning. If you cannot fit them all into the pan, cook in batches on a high heat for a couple of minutes and finish in a medium oven. Serve immediately with a side dish of sauce on each plate. A salad of cucumber seasoned with a good squeeze of lime, and basmati rice with fresh chopped coriander forked through it make good accompaniments.

Navarin of Lamb

Navarin of lamb is traditionally a simple braised dish with carrots, onions and tomato purée. This recipe adds a few extra ingredients to make a far more interesting version.

Utensils Large, shallow 30cm/12in buffet casserole, frying pan

1 tablespoon butter
3 tablespoons olive oil
1.35kg/2¾lb leg of lamb, boned or end of leg
Sea salt and freshly ground black pepper

1 Pre-heat the oven to 170°C/325°F/Gas 3. Melt the butter into the oil in a large shallow pan over a medium heat. Cut the lamb into large 5cm/2in cubes, removing any skin and fat, and brown each piece on both sides. To achieve the right colour, only brown a few pieces at a time. Season.

2 tablespoons flour
2 tablespoons redcurrant jelly
50ml/2fl oz red wine vinegar, aged if obtainable
2 tablespoons tomato purée
400ml/14fl oz stock
225ml/8fl oz red wine

2 When the last few pieces of meat are in the pan, add the rest of the browned meat and the flour and stir for a couple of minutes. Add the redcurrant jelly, vinegar and tomato purée and gradually stir in the stock and red wine over a medium heat.

One medium onion, thinly sliced
3 cloves garlic, crushed
2 teaspoons dried rosemary
2 teaspoons dried thyme
1 bay leaf

3 Add the onion and garlic to the pan with the herbs. Stir well and bring to the boil. Season, cover and cook in the oven for 1 hour.

9 shallots
Knob of butter
4 large carrots

4 Meanwhile, peel and halve the shallots. Melt the butter in a large frying pan and fry the shallots on a high heat until soft, golden and caramelised. Peel and cut the carrots into sticks 1 x 5cm/½ x 2in. After an hour, add the carrots and shallots to the pan and cook for a further 30 minutes, with the lid on.

250g/9oz mange tout, stalks removed.

5 Just before serving, add the mange tout and return the pan to the oven without the lid for two to three minutes.

6 Check the seasoning and serve. Remember the mange tout only take a few minutes to cook and should still be crisp. Serve with Parsley Mash (see page 132).

Top Tip This dish can be re-heated for half an hour in an oven at the same temperature, but only cook the meat for one hour prior to this. Don't re-heat the mange tout.

Preparation and Cooking Time:

1 hour 30 minutes

Beef Stifado

Beef Stifado is a domestic Greek dish. It has a rich sauce with the unique kick of chilli, and the meat is meltingly soft.

Utensils Large buffet casserole, medium frying pan

1kg/2¼lb baby onions
1kg/2¼lb beef shin or braising beef
A little flour
2 tablespoons oil

1 Pour boiling water over the onions and leave to cool – they will then be much easier to peel. Cut the beef into 5cm/2in pieces, dust with flour and fry in the hot oil in small batches until a good dark brown colour. Remove each batch from the pan once it is ready.

600ml/1 pint red wine
3 tablespoons red wine vinegar
1 teaspoon sugar
1 teaspoon salt
1 teaspoon oregano
½ teaspoon chilli flakes
½ teaspoon allspice
4 cloves
2 bay leaves

2 Put all the meat back into the pan, add the wine, vinegar, sugar and all the spices. Bring to a gentle simmer.

2 tablespoons oil
2 cloves garlic
700g/1lb 7oz jar passata
60g/2¼oz sultanas

3 Pre-heat the oven to 180°C/350°F/Gas 4. Peel the onions and fry in hot oil until golden brown. Add the garlic and stir in the passata. Add this to the beef, along with the sultanas. Bring back to a gentle simmer, cover and cook in the oven for 1 hour or cook on a very low heat on the hob. (See note on fan ovens page 7).

4 Serve with parsley potatoes or noodles and wilted spinach.

Top Tip Be sure not to overcook the meat otherwise it will become tough and stringy.

Beef Tagine with Harissa

Although this is a spiced Moroccan dish, the prunes give it a sweet dimension. Try this with Harissa (see page 79) as an accompaniment (harissa is great to have as a standby in your fridge to spice up anything you like).

Utensils Large buffet casserole, electric blender or pestle and mortar

1 kg/2¼lb shin of beef or braising beef
2 tablespoons olive oil
2 tablespoons plain flour

1 Pre-heat the oven to 180°C/350°F/Gas 4. Cut the meat into 5cm/2in squares. Heat the oil in the pan over a medium heat and fry the beef in small batches until a darkish brown. Put the meat back into the pan, add the flour and stir until it reaches a light brown.

2 sticks celery, chopped
2 onions, chopped
2 cloves garlic
1 teaspoon cinnamon
1 teaspoon coriander seeds, ground
1 teaspoon dried chilli flakes
2 bay leaves

2 Add the celery and onions and cook for about 5 minutes. Stir in the garlic followed by the spices. Fry for a couple of minutes to enhance the flavour; then add the bay leaves.

360g/12oz prunes
750ml/1¼ pints hot vegetable stock
Sea salt and freshly ground black pepper

3 Add the prunes and the hot stock, which should just cover the contents of the pan. Bring to the boil, then put in the oven and simmer very gently (see note on fan ovens page 7) for 1 hour until tender. Check seasoning.

Small bunch coriander, chopped for garnish

4 Serve with plenty of coriander, hot couscous and harissa.

Top Tip Always try to buy the braising beef in one piece and cut to size rather than using the pre-packaged meat, which can often be 'cubed' far too small.

Serves lots
Preparation and Cooking Time:
15–20 minutes

Harissa

Utensils Food processor, small baking tray

3 red peppers

1 Remove the skins from the peppers by pre-heating the grill to its highest setting. Cut the peppers in half, remove the seeds, then place the peppers skin-side up on the baking tray under the grill. They will be ready when the skin has blackened. Peel and throw into the food processor.

3 red chillies
2 garlic cloves, peeled
1 teaspoon tomato purée
1 teaspoon ground coriander
4 tablespoons olive oil
Sea salt and freshly ground
black pepper

2 Cut the chillies in half and remove the seeds, then add to the food processor with the garlic, tomato purée, ground coriander and olive oil. Blend to a paste, taste and season.

chapter six

girls just want to have brunch

American-style brunch

is becoming more and more popular these days as people catch on that there really is no better start to the weekend than a leisurely lie-in followed by a relaxing combination of breakfast and lunch. As a way to entertain, most of the following dishes can be prepared in advance and finished off as your friends arrive. Just try to resist our Blueberry Pancakes or Stuffed French Toast! Or if you're feeling virtuous, you could always take the healthy option and go for the juices.

Serves 4 (makes 8 small crab cakes)
Preparation and Cooking Time:
20 minutes

Crab Cakes

Crab is at its best during the late summer months. These little cakes are simple and easy to prepare.

Utensils Food processor for breadcrumbs, large non-stick pan

5 slices white bread

1 Blend the bread in the food processor to make 6 tablespoons of fine breadcrumbs.

225g/8oz brown and white crab meat (about 1½ dressed crabs)
2 tablespoons crème fraîche
2 tablespoons chives, chopped
1 egg
Sea salt and freshly ground black pepper

2 Gently mix the breadcrumbs in a bowl with the rest of the ingredients. Try not to 'overmix' the mixture.

Flour for dusting

3 Sprinkle the flour onto a plate. Take a small round of the crab mixture, roll into a cake shape and then carefully dip in the flour. Keep flat and covered in the fridge if not cooking straight away.

A little oil for frying

4 Heat the pan, add the oil and lightly fry each small cake for a couple of minutes on each side or until light brown. If you cannot fit them all into the pan at once, fry them in batches and keep warm in a low oven.

5 Serve on a warm plate with a little very finely sliced fennel with lemon juice and olive oil or chilli jam (see page 55), or for something more substantial serve with parsley mash (see page 132).

Serves 6–8 as a main course
Preparation and Cooking Time:
20 minutes, plus 2–4 days
marinating

Gravad Lax

Although this uses quite a lot of salmon, it is an excellent recipe for a starter or light main course. The quantities here leave you with enough leftovers to keep refrigerated for many days – perfect for snacking if you don't use it all at once buffet-style.

Utensils Large baking tray, foil, cling film, food processor

1 side from a 3kg/7lb salmon, weighing roughly 1kg/2¼lb

1 The salmon size may seem daunting but a fishmonger will prepare it for you by removing any pin bones. If they haven't, run your finger down the middle of the fillet and remove any remaining bones with tweezers. Find a large baking tray that the salmon will fit into diagonally. Lay a large piece of foil flat onto the tray, leaving enough to wrap around the fillet, and cover this with a layer of cling film.

Large bunch fresh dill
85g/3½oz Maldon salt
175g/6oz caster sugar
Freshly ground black pepper

2 Chop the dill quite finely and mix together the salt, sugar and pepper. Spread half of this in a line where the salmon will lie and then place the salmon skin-side down on top. Spread the remaining mix over the salmon flesh. Wrap well and refrigerate for 2–4 days. Turn the fillet over each day to enable the pickling to 'work' efficiently. During this time a little of the juice will collect on the foil but don't worry.

2 tablespoons Dijon mustard
Small bunch dill
2 tablespoons rice wine vinegar
2 tablespoons olive oil
2 tablespoons double cream

3 Put the mustard and dill into a food processor with the rice wine vinegar and blend, then with the blade still moving slowly, add the oil to make an emulsion. Add the cream and season.

4 To serve, unwrap the salmon – by now the salt and sugar will have dissolved, leaving the salmon perfectly marinated. Slice the salmon thickly and use the extra dill to decorate. Serve the mustard sauce separately along with a dark rye bread and cucumber and dill salad (see page 111).

Top Tip Some supermarkets sell a good ready-made version of the mustard dill sauce.

Stuffed French Toast

This is a variation on the original with a surprise, gooey centre of apricot jam.

Utensils Large frying pan

4 thick slices white bread
2 generous tablespoons good-quality apricot jam or any flavour you fancy

1 Spread the apricot jam evenly over two slices of bread. Place the other bread slices on top and cut each sandwich on the diagonal.

4 eggs
A couple of knobs of butter

2 Break the eggs into a bowl and whisk. Dip each sandwich into the egg and start to heat the butter in a large frying pan. When the butter is foaming, turn the heat down slightly and fry each triangle until a delicate golden brown.

2 teaspoons caster sugar
½ teaspoon cinnamon

3 Serve immediately on warm plates. Top with a sprinkling of cinnamon and sugar.

Meatloaf with Baked Portobello Mushrooms and Fried Eggs

Serves 4

Cooking and Preparation Time:
1 hour 15 minutes

Although this is great for brunch, you can also use it as a simple supper dish.

Utensils Food processor, medium loaf tin, medium pan or frying pan, large mixing bowl, medium high-sided baking tray

Knob of butter
2 medium onions, chopped
2 cloves garlic, crushed
1 heaped tablespoon chopped
fresh thyme
Sea salt and freshly ground
black pepper

1 Pre-heat oven to 190°C/375°F/Gas 5. Melt the butter in the pan and cook the onions for a couple of minutes on a low to medium heat until soft. Add the garlic and thyme and season.

300g/11oz minced beef
300g/11oz minced pork
150g/5oz white bread
5 tablespoons Worcester sauce
5 teaspoons Dijon mustard
3 teaspoons celery seeds

2 Mix together the minced beef and pork. Pulse the bread into fine breadcrumbs in a food processor (this will only take a couple of seconds) and add to the meat along with the Worcester sauce, mustard and celery seeds. Using your hands or a rubber scraper, blend all the ingredients together. Pour into the loaf tin and press down well, leaving an even, flat top. Stand in a baking tray and pour boiling water into the tray as high as you can. Bake for one hour.

4 portobello mushrooms, sliced
thickly
3 heaped tablespoons chopped
fresh tarragon

3 Nearing the end of baking time, prepare the mushrooms by placing them on a large piece of foil on a baking tray. Sprinkle with plenty of seasoning and chopped tarragon, then wrap the foil loosely. Bake for 25 minutes.

Knob of butter
4 medium eggs

4 Heat a little butter in a frying pan until foaming. Break the eggs gently into the pan and turn the heat down low. Season and gently cook until the whites have set.

5 To serve, carefully slice the meatloaf and serve with the mushrooms and eggs on the side.

Camembert Quesadillas with Papaya Salsa and Guacamole

Serves 4 (makes 6 in total)
Preparation and Cooking Time:
30 minutes

Utensils Medium mixing bowl, food processor, large frying pan, small baking tray and palette knife

1 papaya (not too ripe)
1 red onion, finely chopped
1 green chilli, seeds removed
1 tablespoon chopped fresh mint
Juice of 2 limes
Sea salt and freshly ground black pepper

1 To make the salsa, peel the papaya, cut in half lengthways and remove the black seeds with a teaspoon. Slice the fruit thinly (about 5mm/¼in thick), then cut in half and chop into 5mm/¼in squares. Place in a mixing bowl with the onion, chilli and mint and squeeze over the lime juice. Season well and stir gently to mix up all the flavours. Cover and chill.

3 green chillies, seeds removed
45g/1¾oz fresh coriander
3 ripe avocados, peeled and stoned
Juice of 2 limes

2 To make the guacamole, blend the chillies and coriander to a purée in a food processor. Add the avocado flesh and juice of the limes, season well and pulse. The guacamole really does not have to be a smooth purée. Cover and chill.

2 x 240g/8½oz whole Camembert (unripe)
12 x 17cm/6½in flour tortillas

3 Slice the Camembert thinly with rind still attached. Lay six of the tortillas flat and cover with the cheese slices. Top with the remaining tortillas and stack carefully on a plate. Cover with a damp cloth ready for frying.

6 tablespoons sunflower oil
6 tablespoons butter

4 Pre-heat the oven to 140°C/275°F/Gas 1 and warm the plates. Heat 1 tablespoon oil and 1 tablespoon butter in the large frying pan and, when foaming, add a quesadilla and gently fry for two minutes until golden brown. Turn over using a palette knife and fry the other side for a further 2 minutes. Place on the baking tray in the oven to keep warm whilst cooking the other quesadillas, making sure you wipe the pan after each one.

5 To serve, cut the quesadillas into quarters. Serve with a good spoonful of salsa and guacamole.

Kedgeree

Kedgeree originated as a breakfast dish for the British Colonialists in India and is equally popular now as a supper dish. We use mushrooms and fresh fish as well as smoked fish to give a lighter texture and fresher taste.

Utensils 2 large frying pans or 1 large ovenproof dish, coffee grinder or pestle and mortar, 1 medium saucepan and 1 small saucepan

350g/12oz smoked haddock fillet
350g/12oz fresh haddock fillet
A few black peppercorns
1 bay leaf

1 Pre-heat the oven to 180°C/350°F/Gas 4. First poach both fish by placing the fillets skin-side up in a large frying pan or ovenproof dish. Cover with boiling water, add the peppercorns and bay leaf and bring to a simmer. Cover with foil and put in the oven for 15 minutes or until the fish skin is easy to remove. Take the fish out of the water and leave to cool.

1 medium onion, chopped
50g/2oz butter
1 clove garlic
1 teaspoon cumin seeds
1 teaspoon tomato purée
1 teaspoon turmeric
¼ teaspoon fennel seeds
1 teaspoon curry powder
Large pinch of saffron
1 bay leaf

2 To make the curry sauce melt the butter and gently fry the chopped onion in a large frying pan over a low heat. Crush the garlic, grind the cumin (if using whole seeds) in a coffee grinder or using a pestle and mortar and add to the pan; fry for 3 minutes. Add the tomato purée, turmeric, curry powder, saffron, bay leaf and 150ml/¼ pint cold water; simmer for 15 minutes uncovered.

300g/11oz basmati rice
1 teaspoon cumin seeds

3 While the curry sauce is cooking, prepare the basmati rice. Rinse the rice and place in a large saucepan. Cover with boiling water, about 2.5cm/1in above the rice level. Add salt and simmer for 10 minutes. Strain and place back in the same pan. Stir in the cumin seeds. Cover with a tight-fitting lid and leave to steam off the heat for 5–10 minutes.

350g/12oz chestnut mushrooms
3 medium eggs

4 Flake the fish fillets into large chunks and remove any bones, skin, peppercorns and the bay leaf. Chop the mushrooms into quarters. Place the eggs in a saucepan, cover with cold water, bring to the boil and simmer for 6 minutes. Immerse in very cold running water until they are cool, then peel and cut into quarters.

50g/2oz butter
Small bunch flat leaf parsley, chopped
Sea salt and freshly ground black pepper

5 To serve, re-heat the curry sauce over a gentle heat and add the mushrooms, stirring well to cook – this should take 3–4 minutes. Carefully stir in the delicate fish and rice and heat through well for 4–5 minutes. Season well and add the extra butter. Place the eggs on top, scatter with chopped parsley and spoon onto hot plates.

Top Tip Ensure that the rice is well heated – it should be over 65°C/150°F before eating.

Corned Beef Hash

Utensils 1 large non-stick frying pan

4 medium potatoes	**1** Boil the potatoes for 10–12 minutes, drain and cool under cold running water, then grate on a thick grater.
225g/8oz tinned corned beef 1 onion, finely chopped ½ teaspoon dried thyme Sea salt and freshly ground black pepper	**2** Chop the beef roughly, then mix in a large bowl with the potato, onion, thyme and salt and pepper.
2 tablespoons butter 1 tablespoon olive oil	**3** Pre-heat the grill. Heat the butter and olive oil in the frying pan. When foaming, add the potato mixture, pushing it flat into the shape of the pan. Leave to cook on the hob over a medium heat for about 15 minutes.
	4 Using a spatula, gently lift the bottom of the potato to check the colour. When golden brown, place the whole pan under the grill to cook the top side for 3–4 minutes or until the same colour as the bottom.
Small bunch chopped parsley	**5** Cut into thick wedges, season and garnish with the chopped parsley and serve with a fried egg and tomato sauce.

Blueberry Pancakes

Utensils Food processor, large bowl, large non-stick frying pan and whisk

½ teacup milk
1 medium egg
1 medium egg yolk

1 Using a food processor, mix the milk, whole egg and egg yolk together (saving the one spare white to add to the three more whites you'll use later in the recipe).

1 teacup plain flour
½ teaspoon baking powder
½ teaspoon bicarbonate of soda
Pinch of salt

2 Add the flour, baking powder and bicarbonate of soda to the batter mixture. Blend again, add seasoning and pour into a large bowl.

4 egg whites

3 Whisk the egg whites until firm, stir a quarter of them into the mixture, then carefully fold in the rest.

A little sunflower oil for frying
250g/9oz punnet blueberries

4 Pre-heat the oven to 140°C/275°F/Gas 1. Heat a non-stick frying pan with a little sunflower oil over a medium heat. When the oil is hot, spoon a tablespoonful of the pancake mixture into the pan and leave for 2–3 minutes or until the top looks semi-firm and the underside is brown. Add some of the blueberries and use a large spatula to flip the pancake over and fry for a few seconds on the other side. The mixture should make approximately 8 pancakes. Wrap in foil and keep warm in the oven.

Maple syrup (optional)

5 You can just enjoy these on their own or, for a really decadent sweet treat, drizzle over some maple syrup.

Apple Spice Cake

Utensils 26cm/10¼in springform cake tin, electric hand whisk, plastic sieve and plastic scraper

220g/7¾oz butter
340g/12oz light muscovado sugar
2 size 2 eggs

1 Pre-heat the oven to 190°C/375°F/Gas 5. Beat the butter and sugar together in a large bowl until light and fluffy, then beat in the egg.

1 teaspoon vanilla essence
500ml/17fl oz tinned apple purée
350g/12oz plain flour
1 teaspoon ground cinnamon
1 teaspoon nutmeg, ground or freshly grated
good pinch salt
1 teaspoon baking powder
2 teaspoons bicarbonate of soda
220g/7¾oz raisins

2 Add the vanilla and apple purée. Sift in the flour, cinnamon, nutmeg, salt, baking powder and bicarbonate of soda and fold in carefully along with the raisins.

3 Line the bottom of the springform tin with a circle of parchment paper. Spread the mixture into the cake tin and bake for 30–40 minutes or until the sponge springs back when pressed gently.

4 Leave to cool in the tin. Cut around the edge and release the tin sides.

JUICES

All these juices require a juicer – a piece of kitchen equipment we can highly recommend. The freshly extracted juice is not only full of vitamins, minerals and live enzymes, but tastes wonderful and helps you to feel great.

Makes 1 cup
Preparation and Cooking Time:
a few minutes

Charlie's Apple and Carrot Juice

Utensils Juicer

2 thin slices of ginger
1 carrot, chopped
2 apples, cored
3 sprigs fresh mint

1 Process all ingredients together. Mix well and serve.

Makes 1 cup
Preparation and Cooking Time:
a few minutes

Carrot, Orange and Papaya Juice

The carrots provide beta carotene, the papaya and orange Vitamin C.

Utensils Juicer

375g/13oz papaya, peeled, seeded and chopped
1 orange, peeled, seeded and chopped
1 carrot, chopped

1 Process the fruits and the carrot together. Mix well and serve.

Makes 1 cup

Preparation and Cooking Time:
a few minutes

Pineapple Lifter

The enzymes in the pineapple help you to keep alert and aid concentration.

Utensils Juicer

2cm/¾in piece of fresh ginger
½ medium pineapple, peeled, cored and chopped

1 Process the ginger first, then add the pineapple.

½ teaspoon chopped fresh mint

2 Stir in the mint and serve.

Makes 1 cup

Preparation and Cooking Time:
a few minutes

Virgin Mary

Fresh celery juice is delicious as well as being high in potassium to regulate blood pressure.

Utensils Juicer

1 celery stalk with leaves, chopped
160ml/5½fl oz tomato juice, chilled
Splash of Worcester sauce

1 Process the celery and mix with the tomato juice and Worcester sauce. Mix well with ice and serve.

chapter seven

you are what you eat

Let's face it

Most women like to watch their waistline and consequently what they eat at some time or other. This chapter cover recipes that are not only healthy and nutritious but also but also full of flavour.

Aubergine Parmigiana

This is a great vegetarian dish that even meat lovers find hard to resist.

Utensils 2 large baking trays, food processor or hand blender, medium ovenproof dish.

18 plum tomatoes
2 aubergines
Olive oil

1 Pre-heat the oven 200°C/400°F/Gas 6. Cut the tomatoes in half and place on the baking tray, cut-side up. Cut the aubergines into 1cm/½in slices and place on the other baking tray. Drizzle both the tomatoes and aubergine with a little olive oil. Bake for 20 minutes. Remove the aubergine from the oven and cook the tomatoes for a further 10 minutes. Leave the oven on.

2 eggs
50g/2oz Parmesan, grated
250g/9oz ricotta
300g/11oz Mozzarella
Small bunch parsley, roughly chopped
Sea salt and freshly ground black pepper

2 Meanwhile, mix together the eggs, grated Parmesan, ricotta and parsley and season. Cut the Mozzarella into 1cm/½in cubes. Keep this to one side.

2 teaspoons dried oregano

3 Blend the tomatoes, skin and all, to a fine purée. Add the oregano and season. Pour one-third of this sauce into the base of the ovenproof dish, top with a few aubergine slices and add a little seasoning. Dot one-third of the egg and ricotta mix over the aubergines, followed by one-third of the mozzarella. Repeat until all the ingredients are used but on the last layer leave the tomato sauce for the top, layering the cheeses as before.

4 Bake in the oven for 25 minutes until the top is golden brown. Serve with warm herb bread.

Asparagus Salad with Red Pepper Dressing

Serves 4

Preparation and Cooking Time:
40 minutes

Asparagus should only really be used in May, at the beginning of the season when it is young and at its best.

Utensils Food Processor or hand blender, baking tray, large saucepan

3 red peppers

1 Pre-heat the oven to 200°C/400°F/Gas 6. Cut the peppers in half and remove the stalks and seeds. Place on a baking tray and bake for 10 minutes or until blackish around the edges. Cover with cling film and leave to cool slightly. Remove the skins.

1 lemon
4 tablespoons olive oil
Sea salt and freshly ground black pepper

2 Put the pepper flesh into the food processor with the juice from the lemon, the oil and a fair amount of seasoning and blend to a fine purée. A hand blender can be used but you'll get a better result with a food processor. This will leave you with a thick pepper dressing.

1kg/2¼lb asparagus

3 Bring a large pan of salted water to the boil. Cut away the tips of the asparagus, leaving tender 6–7cm/2½–3in pieces and add them to the saucepan. As soon as the water comes back to the boil, take out the asparagus and put them into a bowl of very cold water – this will prevent them from continuing to cook. Drain and keep in reserve until ready to use – they should be only just cooked and still crunchy.

250g/9oz rocket
Balsamic vinegar, preferably an aged variety
Extra virgin olive oil

4 Drizzle the oil and balsamic vinegar over the rocket. Lay on a large plate with the asparagus arranged on top and the pepper dressing poured over. Serve straight away.

Thai Squid Salad

This salad takes quite a bit of preparation but can be thrown together at the last minute. It is a great 'help yourself' starter.

Utensils Large mixing bowl, wok or frying pan, very large serving dish

130g/4½oz rice noodles

1 Follow the instructions for cooking the noodles and leave to cool in iced water.

3 sticks lemongrass
Large bunch fresh coriander
2 red chillies, de-seeded
4 tablespoons fish sauce
2 tablespoons sesame oil
Juice of 1 lime
Sugar, to taste

2 To make the dressing, slice the lemongrass into quarters lengthwise and then chop finely. Chop the coriander and chillies and mix in the large bowl with the sesame oil, lime juice and a little sugar.

300g/11oz beansprouts
1 cucumber
2 medium courgettes
1 bunch spring onions
2 carrots
Sea salt and freshly ground black pepepr

3 If eating immediately, throw the beansprouts into the same bowl along with the rest of the vegetables, but be careful not to dress the salad too early as it will wilt.

Cut the cucumber into 6cm/2½in lengths, then cut away each side, leaving a cube of seeds. Cut the sides into matchstick-shape sticks. Cut the courgettes in the same way. Slice the spring onions on the diagonal and cut the carrots to roughly the same size as the courgettes and cucumber. Stir in the drained noodles. Season well.

4 squid
12 raw tiger prawns
A little sesame oil

4 Cut the squid in half and remove the plastic-looking spine if still intact. Score the halves with a sharp knife and cut into 1.5cm/¾in strips. Shell the prawns. Heat the oil in the pan until smoking and stir-fry the prawns and then the squid for a few minutes. The prawns should be pink and firm and the squid white and curly around the edges. Be careful not to over-cook. Serve on a large plate with the warm prawns and squid thrown over the top.

Top Tip Try to buy the prawns raw with the heads still intact. If you are buying frozen, look for prawns with the shell still on.

Provençal Vegetables with Basil Aïoli

Serves 4
Preparation and Cooking Time:
25 minutes

Rich Provençal flavours have been adapted for this vegetarian dish. It is a one-pot recipe which saves on washing up! Tinned artichoke hearts are fine for this dish.

Utensils Large shallow saucepan

1 medium celeriac, about
380g/13oz
2 medium potatoes
1 fennel bulb
400g/14oz tin artichoke hearts

1 Peel and cut the celeriac and potatoes into 1.5cm/¾in cubes. Cut the fennel in half lengthwise and then into thin strips. Cut the artichokes into quarters.

3 tablespoons olive oil
2 cloves garlic, crushed
1 large pinch saffron
1 teaspoon fennel seeds
3 sprigs thyme
2 bay leaf
2 tablespoons tomato purée
2 tablespoons pastis
225ml/8fl oz white wine
2 cups vegetable stock

2 Heat the olive oil in the large saucepan, add the crushed garlic and then the rest of the ingredients. Bring these to a gentle simmer, season and add the vegetables. Simmer, uncovered, for 20 minutes or until the potatoes and celeriac feel cooked when tested with the tip of a knife.

Small bunch fresh basil
1 clove garlic, crushed
225g/8oz good mayonnaise
Juice of ½ lemon
Sea salt and freshly ground
black pepper

3 Meanwhile, make the aïoli by chopping the basil and mixing with the crushed garlic and mayonnaise. Add the lemon juice and season well.

4 Check the seasoning and ladle the vegetables with plenty of the fragrant liquid into a deep bowl. Serve the aïoli separately, to be spooned on as desired.

Melanie Sykes' Thai Beef Salad

Utensils Frying pan, coffee grinder or pestle and mortar, wok

1 tablespoon Thai fragrant rice

1 Heat a heavy-based frying pan, add the rice and cook over a medium heat for 4–5 minutes. The grains should be an even golden brown. Grind the rice in a clean coffee grinder or pestle and mortar.

450g/1lb beef fillet, approximately 3 small steaks

2 Pre-heat the grill to high and grill the meat for 2–3 minutes on each side close to the heat – it should be quite rare. Slice it thinly and leave to one side.

4 shallots or ½ onion
4 tablespoons fresh coriander, chopped
4 spring onions

3 Chop the shallots and coriander, slice the spring onions and keep to one side.

8 tablespoons beef stock
4 tablespoons fish sauce
Juice of 1 lemon or 1 lime
1 teaspoon crushed dried chillies or chilli powder
2 teaspoons caster sugar

4 Put the stock, fish sauce, lemon juice, chilli and caster sugar into a wok and bring to the boil. Add the beef and stir in the shallots, spring onions, chopped coriander and rice. Stir and heat for a few seconds only. Serve with a green salad or a cucumber and lime salad and steamed rice.

Smoked Chicken and Orange Salad

This is a great summer salad. The unique flavour of the smoked chicken makes it definitely worth hunting for, and some supermarkets do stock it. If you need a little something extra with this salad, try a warm herb bread (see page 19). The chicken and orange will keep for the next day, but once the dressing is on the salad it should be eaten straightaway.

Utensils   Large serving dish

500g/1lb 1½oz smoked chicken breasts
1 orange

1   Cut the chicken into rough 2cm/¾in cubes and place in a mixing bowl. Zest and chop the orange and add to the chicken. Using a bread knife, cut the ends from the orange and then following the curved line cut away the peel. By holding the orange in one hand over the bowl, cut each segment, removing all pith.

3 tablespoons olive oil
½ tablespoon white wine vinegar
2 tablespoons water
Sea salt and freshly ground black pepper

2   Mix the dressing ingredients in a separate bowl with 2 tablespoons of water and drizzle over the chicken and orange.

120g/4½oz rocket
2 Little Gem lettuce, thinly sliced
Small bunch flat leaf parsley
Small bunch chives, some chopped and some whole

3   Place the rocket, lettuce and parsley on a large serving dish, drizzle with the dressing and season well. Place the chicken in the middle and sprinkle with the chives.

Sea Bass with Asian Greens

This is an adaptation of an Alastair Little recipe. Bass is particularly good to use in this recipe as once cooked, its skin will be crispy and the white flesh succulent. If you want to substitute another fish use sole, turbot, halibut or brill (their flesh does not break up during cooking either). Bass is not in season from January through to June.

Utensils Grater, mixing bowl, tweezers, large frying pan with metal handle, wok and palette knife

2 tablespoons soy sauce
1 lemon, juiced
1 teaspoon grated fresh ginger
1 clove garlic, chopped
2 red chillies, deseeded and thinly sliced

1 In a bowl, mix together the soy sauce, lemon juice, ginger, garlic and chillies.

150g/5oz pak choi leaves
200g/7oz baby spinach leaves
1 bunch spring onions
125g/4 1/2oz shiitake mushrooms

2 Slice the pak choi into thick 2cm/3/4in pieces. Wash the spinach. Cut the spring onions diagonally into 1cm/1/2in slices and thinly slice the mushrooms. Preheat the oven to 200°C/400°F/Gas 6.

4 x 225g/8oz sea bass fillets
A little seasoned flour

3 Trim the sea bass fillets and check that all the bones have been removed. Tweezers can be used to remove any rogue bones. Sprinkle a little seasoned flour onto each fillet. If serving rice, cook it now.

75g/3oz butter

4 Melt 50g/2oz butter in a large frying pan. When hot, add the fish, skin side down, and leave for 3 minutes. Then place the whole pan in the oven for 5 minutes. If you don't have a pan that can go directly into the oven, use a heated baking tray.

Sea salt and freshly ground black pepper

5 While the fish is cooking, heat a wok. Add the pak choi, spring onions, spinach and mushrooms, and simply pour over the soy mix. Season and stir fry until the spinach has wilted and the mushrooms are cooked, then add the remaining butter.

To Serve:
A little chilli oil and rice

6 When the vegetables have wilted and the sauce has reduced a little, season and spoon onto warm plates. Using a palette knife, place the fish on top of the vegetables. If wished, a little chilli oil can be drizzled over. This can be served with rice.

Kate Winslet's Salmon Teriyaki Style

This is Kate's version of Salmon Teriyaki. It is delicious, light and healthy, and Kate suggests it is served with a good quality red onion relish. You can also serve it with some rice if you wish.

Utensils Glass or china dish to marinate

2 salmon steaks
100ml/3½fl oz Japanese soy sauce
100ml/3½fl oz dry sherry
100ml/3½fl oz balsamic vinegar
40g/1½ oz caster sugar
Pinch of dried crushed red chillies
Juice of ½ a lemon
1 teaspoon fresh thyme leaves
3–4 tablespoons sunflower oil
Sea salt and freshly ground black pepper

1 Wipe the steaks and place in bowl with a lid. Mix all the marinade ingredients together and add to the salmon. Cover and leave for 1 hour to marinate.

2 Remove the steaks from the marinade, brush with oil and barbecue or grill on a medium heat for 3–4 minutes on each side. The fish is cooked when the flesh flakes.

Red onion relish and lime or lemon wedges to garnish

3 Serve with red onion relish and lime or lemon wedges.

Chicken Basquaise

This is a variation on an Elizabeth David classic Spanish recipe. It can be easily made, thrown in the oven and forgotten about. You will only need to think about the accompaniments.

Utensils 1 large buffet casserole

4 corn-fed chicken legs and 2 breasts
A good knob of butter

1 Chop off the knobbly ends of the chicken legs using the heal of a heavy sharp knife; cut the breasts in half across the middle. Melt the butter in a buffet casserole and, when the butter is hot and foaming, fry the chicken a few pieces at a time until brown. Remove from the pan and keep to one side.

A little olive oil
1 onion
1 clove garlic
3 large sprigs fresh marjoram, leaves removed
1 dessertspoon smoked paprika

2 Add a little olive oil to the pan and fry the onion over a medium heat until soft. Add the garlic, marjoram and paprika. Stir and fry for a few seconds to enhance the flavour.

1 glass white wine
400g/14oz tin tomatoes
400g/14oz pimento, roughly chopped
2 strips orange peel
2 bay leaves
160g/5¼oz chorizo, chopped

3 Pre-heat the oven to 190°C/375°F/Gas 4. Add the wine, tinned tomatoes and pimento. Throw in the orange peel and bay leaves; stir well and bring back to a simmer. Add the chicken legs, chorizo and seasoning. When simmering, cover and cook in the oven for 20 minutes. Then add the breasts and cook for a further 15 minutes.

4 Serve with parsley mash (see page 132) and a green vegetable or green salad. The whole dish can be placed on the table for every one to help themselves – perfect for a girls' night in with a video!

on the
side

Many vegetable recipes

not only stand up well on their own but can transform a simple piece of grilled fish or meat into a delicious and interesting meal when you're strapped for time. Try to use seasonal vegetables and find the freshest available to ensure the best flavour. Don't worry about getting the exact ingredients if they aren't easy to come by – experiment with all types as vegetables are very versatile.

Wild Rice Salad

Although this dressing needs a little bit of preparation, it is well worth the effort. Pomegranate syrup is readily available in specialist sections of supermarkets. Experiment by using it in other recipes – its unique, sharp, lemony flavour is fantastic.

Utensils 1 small saucepan, 1 medium saucepan

3 tablespoons pomegranate syrup
2 tablespoons orange juice
4 tablespoons olive oil
1cm/½in piece fresh ginger
½ clove garlic, crushed
½ red onion, finely chopped
Small bunch fresh coriander, chopped
½ fresh green chilli, seeds removed and chopped
½ teaspoon cumin, ground

Salt
225g/8oz long grain rice
100g/4oz wild rice

1   Pour all the dressing ingredients into a jar and shake to blend.

2   Fill both pans with salted water and bring to the boil. Cook each type of rice separately – the long grain rice will take roughly 10 minutes and the wild rice 30 minutes. When cooked, drain and immerse in cold water, then drain well again.

3   Combine the rice and the dressing, then season. Serve in a large bowl with fish or grilled meat.

Bean Salad with Moroccan Dressing

Utensils Mixing bowl, large saucepan, whisk

2 lemons – 1 zested and 2 juiced
1¼ teaspoons Tabasco
1 clove garlic, chopped
120ml/4fl oz olive oil
1 teaspoon coriander seeds, ground
½ teaspoon mustard powder
2 teaspoons sugar
Sea salt and freshly ground black pepper

1 Whisk together the lemon juice, zest, Tabasco, garlic, olive oil, coriander, mustard and sugar. Add the seasoning.

200g/7oz fine French beans

2 Bring a large pan of salted water to the boil and cook the beans for 3-4 minutes. Immerse in cold water, drain and mix with the dressing. Season again.

3 Serve cold or at room temperature. You can also leave this wrapped in cling film in the fridge to allow the flavours to do their stuff!

Cucumber and Dill Salad

Serves 4

Preparation and Cooking Time:
15 minutes

Possibly one of the easiest salads around. It can be made well in advance, which actually enhances its flavour.

Utensils Small saucepan, high-sided dish

1 large cucumber

100ml/3½fl oz rice wine vinegar
100g/4oz caster sugar

Small bunch dill
Sea salt and freshly ground black pepper

1 Peel and slice the cucumber as thinly as you can.

2 Heat the vinegar in a small pan over a low heat and gradually stir in the sugar until it has dissolved. Remove from the heat and leave to cool.

3 Meanwhile, finely chop the dill, stalks and all. Layer a quarter of the cucumber into a small high-sided dish. Season and sprinkle a quarter of the dill over the cucumber. Repeat until all the ingredients have been used up, seasoning as you go. Pour over the vinegar liquid. Cover and leave for at least one hour (you can in fact leave it overnight).

4 Serve chilled with any fish dish, especially Gravad Lax (see page 84).

Roasted Cauliflower Mash

Serves 4
Preparation and Cooking Time:
20 minutes

Roasting and puréeing the cauliflower gives this recipe a unique and unusual twist.

Utensils Large baking tray, hand blender or food processor

1 medium cauliflower

1 Pre-heat the oven to 200°C/400°F/Gas 6. Cut the cauliflower in half through the core, removing the outer green leaves. Then cut each half into four medium size pieces.

2–3 tablespoons olive oil
Sea salt and freshly ground black pepper

2 Drizzle the oil over the baking tray and heat in the oven for a few minutes. When good and hot, lay the cauliflower pieces flat onto the tray, season well and roast for 20 minutes.

3 When cooked, the cauliflower pieces should have acquired a brown tinge around the edges. While hot, blend the cauliflower using a food processor or hand blender. Season well and serve.

Top Tip This dish can be made in advance and re-heated in the microwave.

Creamed Aubergine Salad

This Middle Eastern dish could be served as an accompaniment or as part of mezze starter, with Hummus (see page 42), Baba Ganoush (see page 43) and flat bread.

Utensils Medium baking tray, food processor

3 aubergines

1 Pre-heat the oven to 190°C/375°F/Gas 5. When ready, place the aubergines on the baking tray and bake for 20 minutes. Remove and leave to cool.

3 tablespoons olive oil
1 lemon
1 clove garlic, crushed
300ml/10fl oz natural yoghurt
Sea salt and freshly ground black pepper

2 When cool, cut the aubergines in half and scoop the soft pulp straight into the food processor. Blend for a few minutes and add the rest of the ingredients. Season well and blend again.

2 tablespoons flat leaf parsley, chopped

3 Pour into a serving dish and garnish with chopped parsley. Serve warm or at room temperature.

Top Tip For a variation, add a couple of spoonfuls of Harissa (see page 79).

Rosti Potatoes

Rosti potatoes are very versatile and can be served as a breakfast dish with eggs or as a quick supper dish with a grilled piece of meat or fish. Try them with pan fried calves' liver with balsamic vinegar and sage.

Utensils Grater, large non-stick frying pan, baking tray for keeping the potatoes warm

450g/1lb Red Desiree potatoes

1 Peel the potatoes and simmer whole in a large saucepan of water for 12 minutes. Strain and leave to cool.

2 tablespoons chives, chopped
25g/1oz butter, melted
Sea salt and freshly ground black pepper

2 Grate the potatoes into a large mixing bowl, add the chopped chives and melted butter, and season. Mix and shape into 8 small 7.5cm/3in rounds.

A little extra butter for frying

3 Using a non-stick frying pan, fry both sides of the potato rounds in a little butter until golden brown. Keep them warm in the oven while you are preparing any accompaniments.

Top Tip Don't make Rosti Potatoes too far in advance as they are only partially cooked at the frying stage and consequently they will discolour slightly. They'll also lose their crispness if they aren't eaten soon after being cooked.

Hassleback Potatoes

This is adapted from an Alistair Little recipe. It makes a great alternative to roast potatoes and can be prepared then simply left in the oven.

Utensils Shallow ovenproof dish

4 large potatoes, about
900g/2lb

1 Pre-heat the oven to 200C/400F/Gas 6. Prepare the potatoes by peeling and cutting in half lengthways. Then slice downwards without slicing right through. The potato shape will be still intact but almost completely sliced through.

6 cloves garlic
85g/3¼oz butter
4 tablespoons olive oil
Sea salt and freshly ground
black pepper

2 Scatter the unpeeled garlic cloves over the base of the dish. Put the potatoes on top, sliced-side upwards. Dot with the butter and drizzle with the oil. Season and cook in the oven for one hour. Baste with the oils as often as you can, but do not try to move the potatoes until cooked.

3 Serve directly from the dish, along with the baked garlic.

Serves 4

Preparation and Cooking Time:
5–10 minutes

Celeriac Remoulade

This makes a great crisp salad to accompany cold meat or for a picnic or lunchbox.

Utensils Food processor with julienne cutter, large saucepan

1 celeriac, peeled

1 Cut the celeriac into small matchstick-size pieces either using a food processor or by hand. If it is chopped by hand, cut it first into thin slices then into strips. Meanwhile bring a large pan of water to the boil. Put in the celeriac and cook for two minutes. Drain and immerse in cold water; drain again and dry.

1½ tablespoons Meaux mustard
1½ tablespoons mayonnaise
1 tablespoon crème fraîche
1 tablespoon natural yoghurt
2 tablespoons fresh tarragon, chopped
Sea salt and freshly ground black pepper

2 Mix together all the ingredients for the dressing, season well and combine with the celeriac.

Top Tip Do blanch the celeriac quite quickly as it tends to turn brown.

Crispy Courgettes

This simple fried vegetable dish seems to be a perennial favourite, particularly with men in Italian restaurants! The courgettes are coated in light batter and consequently the flavour is retained.

Utensils Deep fat fryer or large saucepan

1 litre/1¾ pints sunflower oil

1 Begin to heat the oil in the fryer or pan – it needs to reach 190°C. Make sure you only fill the pan one-third full.

2 large courgettes

2 Cut the courgette into about 3–4cm/1¼–1½in pieces, then cut each side leaving a square of core. Cut these edges into about 3 strips, 5mm/¼in square.

4 tablespoons milk
4 tablespoons flour
Sea salt and freshly ground black pepper

3 Pour the milk onto one plate and the flour, mixed with a good pinch of salt, onto another. Roll the strips of courgette first in the milk and then in the flour.

4 Carefully throw a piece of bread into the oil – if it turns brown after 1 minute, the fat is ready. Gently place the courgettes into the oil and fry for just a few minutes until golden brown.

5 Pour onto kitchen paper, season with salt and serve straightaway.

Top Tip Once the courgettes have been floured they should be fried straightaway. They don't like hanging around!

Serves 4

Preparation and Cooking Time:
20 minutes

Minted Mushy Peas

This makes a good alternative to frozen peas and is great with fish.

Utensils Food processor, medium saucepan

½ an onion
450g/1lb bag frozen petit pois

1 Half-fill the pan with salted water and bring to the boil. Chop the onion finely and throw into the pan with the peas. Bring back to the boil and gently simmer for 5–10 minutes. Drain, put in the food processor and blend to a fine purée.

Small bunch mint, stalks removed
Sea salt and freshly ground black pepper

2 Add the mint leaves and a good amount of seasoning. Blend again. Serve straight from the blender or reheat and use later.

Serves 4

Preparation and Cooking Time:
10 minutes

Cherry Tomato and Basil Salad

This dish can be made in advance and left to chill covered in the fridge.

Utensils Food processor

500g/1lb 1½oz pomodorino or cherry tomatoes
Sea salt and freshly ground black pepper

1 Cut half of the tomatoes in half and mix with the rest, which are left whole. Pour into a serving dish and season.

Small bunch fresh basil
100ml/3½fl oz olive oil

2 Whizz the basil in the food processor and gradually drizzle in the oil to make a thick dressing. Season and pour over the tomatoes; stir to coat well.

Risotto Milanese

Utensils Buffet casserole or large saucepan, medium saucepan and ladle

1 onion
2 tablespoons olive oil

1   Chop the onion finely, heat the oil in the pan and gently fry.

1 litre/1¾ pints vegetable stock
2 large pinches saffron

2   Make the stock to the instructions on the side of the packet, and while still hot add the saffron to infuse. Pour into a saucepan and heat to a gentle simmer.

350g/12oz risotto rice
½ glass white wine

3   Stir the rice into the onion and coat it in oil. Add a couple of ladles of the hot stock and the wine to the rice, stir until absorbed. Continue to stir, adding each ladle of stock gradually until all the stock has been used and the texture of the rice is creamy and soft but still holding its shape. This should take roughly 20 minutes. If it is still hard in the middle, add more stock and continue to cook.

85g/3¼oz Parmesan Reggiano
Sea salt and freshly ground
black pepper

4   When ready stir in the cheese and season. Taste to check, then serve.

Serves 4
Preparation and Cooking Time:
12–15 minutes

Caesar Salad

This is a popular salad dish that is very simple to make. There are many different variations on this classic, but once you've tried our cheat's dressing, you won't go back to buying the bottled ones.

Utensils Baking tray, mixing bowl, grater, large bowl or shallow serving dish

About 4 tablespoons olive oil
50g/2oz bread chunks, torn from a crusty white loaf (each chunk should be about 4cm/1½in)

1 Pre-heat the oven to 200°C/400°F/Gas 6. To make the croûtons, pour the oil onto a baking tray and roll the bread chunks in it. Bake in the oven for 10 minutes, remove and leave to cool.

275ml/½ pint goo- quality mayonnaise
½ lemon, juiced
1 large clove garlic, crushed

2 For the dressing, mix together the mayonnaise, lemon juice and garlic in a mixing bowl. If necessary, add a little cold water to dilute the dressing to the consistency of double cream.

6 Little Gem lettuces

3 Cut the core away from the bottom of the lettuces so the leaves automatically come away. Wash and dry them carefully.

175g/6oz Parmigiano Reggiano cheese
Sea salt and freshly ground black pepper

4 Grate the cheese and add just over half of it to the dressing, reserving the rest for sprinkling, then season.

Small bunch fresh chives, chopped

5 Place a layer of lettuce leaves in a large bowl or shallow serving dish, drizzle with the dressing, sprinkle with some cheese and season. Repeat until all the leaves have been used. Drizzle the top layer with dressing, throw on the croûtons, top with chopped chives and the remaining cheese.

Serves 4
Preparation and Cooking Time:
25–30 minutes

Gratin of Leeks

This is a new take on an old classic dish. Leeks go perfectly with roast meat and are at their best in January and February.

Utensils Large Saucepan, medium ovenproof baking dish

4 leeks

1 Pre-heat the oven to 190°C/375°F/Gas 5. Slice the leeks into thin rounds, removing the root and the very green ends. Wash thoroughly and then throw into a pan of salted water. Leave to boil for a couple of minutes, drain, then cover with cold water and drain again.

5 sprigs thyme
142ml/5fl oz double cream
Sea salt and freshly ground black pepper

2 Pick the thyme leaves from the stalks and chop. In the saucepan bring the cream to the boil and add the leeks and thyme. Season well. Bring back to the boil and then pour into an ovenproof dish.

2 tablespoons breadcrumbs
5 tablespoons grated strong cheese

3 Sprinkle over the mixed cheese and breadcrumbs and bake for 20 minutes until the top is golden brown. Serve with roast lamb or chicken.

Marinated Mushroom Salad

Serves 4

Preparation and Cooking Time:

15 minutes

This is an adaptation of an Elizabeth David recipe. True to her style, it is simple and effective. Great with roast chicken.

Utensils Medium sized serving dish

225g/8oz chestnut mushrooms
Juice of 1 lemon
A few good glugs of a light olive oil
1 clove garlic, chopped
Sea salt and freshly ground black pepper
Small bunch flat leaf parsley

1 Slice the mushrooms into thinnish slices and place in a large serving dish. Squeeze over the lemon juice and drizzle with the olive oil. Add the chopped garlic, parsley and seasoning. Stir well and cover until ready to use.

A few sprigs sweet marjoram, leaves picked from the stalk
A few sprigs lemon thyme, leaves picked from the stalk
More olive oil

2 To serve, add the chopped herbs and another drizzle of olive oil, taste to check if more seasoning is needed.

Roast Baby Beets with Walnut Oil

Beets are in season during the summer and autumn months. Look out for the baby ones which are full of flavour. For some reason they tend to be ignored but are definitely worth a try.

Utensils Large roasting tin

1kg/2½lb baby beetroots
3 tablespoons walnut oil
Sea salt and freshly ground
black pepper

1 Pre-heat the oven to 190°C/375°F/Gas 5. Wash and trim the beets, place on the roasting tray, drizzle with the oil, season and roast for 20 minutes.

3 cloves garlic

2 Throw in the garlic cloves and roast for another 15–20 minutes, until the beets are just done.

A little more walnut oil
Juice of 1 lemon

3 Take the roasted cloves of garlic and squeeze out the soft and mellow insides into a bowl. Whisk in a little more walnut oil, squeeze in the lemon juice and season.

Chopped chives

4 Drizzle the dressing over the beets while they are still warm and serve with a few chopped chives.

Panzanella

If you have a Greek or Turkish supermarket near you, you'll find they sell celery with an abundance of leaves – some supermarkets now sell this kind of celery too. Add as many celery leaves to this crisp Mediterranean salad as you can, because it's the leaves that give it its unique flavour. You can also try using Cabernet red wine vinegar – its flavour is much richer and fuller and not quite as sharp as that of ordinary red wine vinegar.

Utensils Small baking tray

4 medium ripe vine tomatoes
1 medium cucumber
1 medium red onion
1 celery stick, with as many leaves as possible
Small bunch fresh basil, torn into small pieces
Sea salt and freshly ground black pepper
2 tablespoons red wine vinegar

1 Chop the tomatoes roughly, leaving the skin on. Chop the cucumber and onion, and slice the celery and put in a large bowl. Mix well and add the basil. Season and add the vinegar. Cover and marinate for as long as you can, preferably for at least 2 hours.

1 small baguette (it doesn't have to be fresh, it's actually better a day old)
6 tablespoons olive oil

2 Pre-heat the oven to 220°C/425°F/Gas 7. Cut the baguette into thick slices, drizzle with olive oil, place on a baking tray in the oven for 5 minutes. Remove and leave to cool.

Extra virgin olive oil to drizzle

3 Break the bread into 2.5cm/1in pieces and add to the chopped vegetables. Drizzle with a generous amount of olive oil, season well and serve.

Basmati Rice

Still a mystery for some, here is a simple method for basmati rice that simply cannot fail.

Utensils Large saucepan

200g/7oz basmati rice
Sea salt

1 Rinse the rice in a strainer and place in a large saucepan. Cover with boiling water 2.5cm/1in above the rice level. Add salt and simmer for 10 minutes. Strain and place back into the same pan. Cover with a tightly fitting lid and leave to steam for 10 minutes.

2 Gently fork through to separate the grains and serve. Each grain should still have its shape but will be just cooked.

Top Tip Once the lid goes on the rice it can be kept for up to 30 minutes. Always ensure that the rice is kept at a temperature of 65°C before eating. Any leftovers should be thrown away and not re-heated.

chapter nine

tea and sympathy

There is something particularly comforting

about consoling yourself with food. Whether you're feeling the strain from too much partying, miserable because he's calling the shots or just plain fed-up, eating comfort food can instantly help ease the pain. Mushrooms on Toast will help get you back on track after a night on the town and when things are looking truly grim, what goes better with a nice cup of tea than home-made Chocolate Brownies?

Mushrooms on Toast

This makes a delicious, easy and filling snack which is pretty healthy too. Serve as it stands or to accompany a grilled piece of meat or fish for something more substantial.

Utensils 1 large frying pan

Large knob of butter
140g/4¾oz chestnut
mushrooms, thickly sliced
3 medium portobello
mushrooms, thickly sliced
150g/5oz baby chestnut
mushrooms, halved
Sea salt and freshly ground
black pepper

1 Melt the butter in the frying pan, throw in the mushrooms and leave on a medium heat, stirring occasionally. Season.

2 thick slices white bread

2 Meanwhile start to toast the bread.

3–4 sprigs tarragon
1 dessertspoon crème fraîche
Juice of ½ lemon

3 Chop the tarragon and mix with the crème fraîche and lemon juice and stir into the mushrooms. Check the seasoning. At this stage the mushrooms should be wilted and soft.

4 To serve, pile up the mushrooms on the warm bread.

Serves 4

Preparation and Cooking Time:

35 minutes

Minced Beef en Croûte

This is very tasty but needs a little time and attention.

Utensils Large Saucepan or frying pan, rolling pin, large baking tray, pastry brush

1 onion
1 red pepper
2 tablespoons olive oil

1 Chop the onion and pepper finely. Heat the oil in the pan and fry the onion until lightly coloured. Add the pepper and fry for a further couple of minutes.

450g/1lb minced beef
2 tablespoons tomato ketchup
2 teaspoons soy sauce

2 Add the minced beef and use a wooden spoon to break it up; fry gently. Add the ketchup and soy sauce and simmer for 10 minutes. Take the pan off the heat and allow it to cool down.

230g/8oz packet ready-made
butter puff pastry
A little flour

3 While the meat is cooling, roll out the pastry to 25 x 40cm/10 x 16in – use a little flour to dust the work surface. The pastry should be roughly 2mm/⅛in thick.

1 egg, beaten
A few sprinkles of sesame seeds

4 Heat the oven to 200°C/400°F/Gas 6. Lay the pastry on the baking tray and spoon the meat mixture down the centre. Brush along the pastry edges with beaten egg, fold the pastry sides over the meat and gently push together to seal. Turn carefully so the join is on the underside. Brush over with egg and make diagonal slits in the pastry about 5cm/2in apart along the top. Sprinkle with a few sesame seeds and bake for 20 minutes.

5 Serve immediately with a crisp green salad and new potatoes with butter and chives.

Top Tip Once you have your pastry 'parcel' ready, it can be kept covered in the fridge until needed.

Denise Van Outen's Sausages in Cider with Lemon Thyme

Serves 4
Preparation and Cooking Time:
1 hour 15 minutes

A comforting winter warmer. Try to buy good-quality sausages made from outdoor-reared pigs. Perry is a sparkling pear-based wine similar to Babycham. It can be quite difficult to find but is becoming more popular.

Utensils Medium frying pan, large buffet casserole

12 sausages, about 800g/1¾lb
½ tablespoon sunflower oil

1 Heat the oil in a frying pan on a low to medium heat and fry the sausages until light brown.

½ tablespoon sunflower oil
1 medium onion, one half chopped finely, the other half sliced
1 clove garlic, crushed and chopped
1 tablespoon flour

2 Remove the sausages from the pan. Add the additional oil along with the onion and fry lightly until soft. Stir in the garlic, then the flour and leave to cook for a couple of minutes.

225ml/7½fl oz dry cider or perry
½ tablespoon sunflower oil
3 Granny Smith apples, peeled and cut into quarters, core removed and sliced thickly
1 tablespoon fresh chopped lemon thyme
200ml/7fl oz apple juice

3 Add the cider gradually and continue to stir over a low heat, bringing it to a simmer. Meanwhile, heat the oil in a separate pan and fry the sliced apple, which will caramelise quite quickly. Add the apple to the pan of cider, along with the sausages, chopped thyme and apple juice.

4 Season, cover with a lid and simmer gently for one hour, by which time the apples and onions will have become meltingly soft. The aroma will be divine.

Sea salt and freshly ground black pepper

5 To serve, check the seasoning and serve with another comfort food such as mash.

Parsley Mash

This is great served with Minced Beef en Croûte (see page 130) and provides real comfort.

Utensils Medium saucepan, masher

900g/2lb Maris Piper or any white potatoes

1 Peel the potatoes, cut them in half if they are large and place in a medium saucepan. Cover with cold salted water and boil for 20–25 minutes.

Large bunch flat leaf parsley
225ml/8fl oz full fat milk
Large knob of butter
3 tablespoons double cream
Sea salt and freshly ground black pepper

2 Chop the parsley roughly. When the potatoes are soft, drain them and put them back into the pan and leave to steam for a couple of seconds. Mash well and add the milk, butter and cream. Continue to mash until all lumps have been removed. Season, then add the parsley and stir well.

3 Serve immediately or keep warm in a low oven, covered with a lid or foil.

Steak Sandwich

Utensils Large frying pan

Long, very fresh white loaf or baguette

1 Using a bread knife, cut 4 medium slices from the loaf lengthways.

1 onion
Light olive oil

2 Cut the onion in half, peel and slice thinly. Heat the oil in the pan and start to fry the onions on a low heat until soft.

500g/1lb 1½oz thinly sliced fillet or rib eye steak
Sea salt and freshly ground black pepper

3 Lay the beef slices on a flat surface and season well. By this time the onions should be cooked. Cover two of the bread slices with the cooked onions and season well. Turn the heat up, add a little more oil and fry each side of the meat very quickly and put straight on top of the onions. Cover with the slices of bread. Enjoy.

Roberta's Chicken and Leek Pie

This is a real winter warmer and doesn't take too much effort as we cheat by using ready-made puff pastry! You can also use ready cooked chicken. Bear in mind that leeks are at their best from January to March. Try adding any herbs you may have for extra flavour.

Utensils Rolling pin, mixing bowl, 2 medium saucepans, oval stoneware medium pie dish, pastry brush

600g/1lb 6oz leeks, cleaned and sliced into 2.5cm/1in pieces
25g/1oz butter
Splash of white wine (optional)
Sea salt and freshly ground black pepper

1 Pre-heat the oven to 200°C/400°F/Gas 6. Sweat the leeks for 6–7 minutes in a saucepan with the butter and a splash of white wine. Season. Drain and reserve the liquid, as you'll be adding it to the white sauce in the next step.

50g/2oz butter
3 heaped tablespoons flour
300ml/½ pint full fat milk
300ml/½ pint good-quality chicken stock (also use juices from cooked leeks)
2 heaped tablespoons crème fraîche or double cream

2 Meanwhile, make the white sauce. Melt the butter in a saucepan over a medium heat. Stir in the flour off the heat, then replace on the heat and gradually add the milk and stock until the sauce is glossy. Take off the heat and, once the leeks are cooked, stir in the leek juices and the crème fraîche or cream. Season.

1kg/2¼lb chicken, cooked and cut in bite-sized chunks, or 8 boneless thighs

3 Add the leeks to the sauce and then add the chicken, mixing well. Put in the base of the pie dish.

230g/8oz sheet ready-made puff pastry
A little flour
1 egg, beaten

4 Make a pastry rim around the edge of the pie dish and moisten both the underside (so that it sticks to the dish rim) and the topside with milk. Roll out the puff pastry to cover the pie dish, place on top and seal by pressing the pastry to the pastry rim. Mark the edges with a fork, decorate as desired with pastry 'leaves' or twisted strips. Brush over some beaten egg, make a small slit in the pastry centre to release the steam and bake in the oven for about 35 minutes or until the pastry is golden brown.

Pea and Bacon Risotto

Utensils 1 large saucepan, 1 medium saucepan

200g/7oz pancetta, cut into small cubes, or streaky bacon
1 onion, chopped
350g/12oz Carnaroli risotto rice

1 Heat the large pan on a medium heat and add the pancetta. As the fat from the pancetta melts into the pan, add the onion. Stir and leave to cook and caramelise a little. Stir in the rice until well coated in fat.

1.5 litres/2½ pints vegetable stock
½ glass white wine

2 Pour the stock into the medium saucepan and bring to a gentle simmer. It is important to maintain the same heat for the stock throughout the cooking process so that when it's added to the rice, it continues to cook the rice evenly. Add the wine to the rice. Stir as it evaporates a little then gradually add a ladle of the stock to the rice and stir until absorbed. Continue to stir, adding each ladle of stock gradually. This should take about 20 minutes depending on the rice.

175g/6oz frozen peas
110g/4¼oz Parmesan cheese, plus an extra 50g/2oz for shavings
Sea salt and freshly ground black pepper

3 Test the rice: it should be soft but still hold its shape. It should have a little bite, but if it is hard in the middle, add more stock and continue to cook. With the last ladle of stock, stir in the peas and then add the Parmesan. At this stage of cooking the risotto should be quite runny. Check the seasoning and serve.

Choc Chip Cookies

You don't have to eat these all at once – the uncooked sausage shapes can be frozen and defrosted when needed.

Utensils Small saucepan, electric whisk, large baking tray

350g/12oz good-quality chocolate, 60% cocoa solids, broken into small pieces
60g/2¼oz butter

1 Melt the chocolate and butter in the small saucepan on a low heat, or place in a bowl, cover with cling film and melt in the microwave.

4 eggs
135g/4¾oz caster sugar

2 Whisk the eggs and sugar together in a bowl until pale and thick – this should take about 10 minutes.

60g/2¼oz plain flour
15g/½oz baking powder

3 Gently fold in the flour, baking powder and cooled chocolate mixture.

100g/4oz chopped walnuts
300g/11oz choc chips

4 Add the walnuts and choc chips and continue to fold everything together gently.

5 Fold a piece of cling film into double thickness and lay flat on a work surface. Spoon a large sausage shape of the cookie mixture about 20cm/8in long onto the cling film. Roll tightly and twist the ends. The mixture should make about four 'sausages'. Chill in the fridge for about 30 minutes until hard.

6 Pre-heat the oven to 180°C/350°F/Gas 4. Using a sharp knife, cut the roll into 5mm/¼in slices to make the cookies and place on a baking tray. Cook for 5 minutes and leave to cool on the tray.

Chocolate Brownies

Although the thought of lard going into something like this may sound a little strange, it does actually work as it gives that vital chewy texture. These brownies will keep in an air tight container.

Utensils 20cm/8in square cake tin (shallow or deep), greaseproof paper, small saucepan, electric hand whisk or whisk

60g/2½oz good-quality chocolate, 60% cocoa solids, broken into small pieces
75g (3oz) shortening/lard

1 Pre-heat the oven to 350°F/190°C/Gas 5. Grease the tin with fat, then cut a square of greaseproof paper to fit neatly in the bottom. Break the chocolate into a small saucepan and melt with the shortening or lard over a low heat.

2 eggs
250g/9oz caster sugar

2 Whisk the eggs and sugar together in a bowl until light in colour and texture.

90g/3½oz plain flour
½ teaspoon baking powder
pinch of salt
120g/4½oz shelled walnuts

3 Add the melted chocolate mixture to the bowl. Sieve in the flour, baking powder and salt, stir and fold together, being careful not to over-mix (it's best to use a plastic bowl scraper). Before it is completely mixed, stir in the walnuts.

4 Spread evenly into the prepared cake tin and bake in the middle of the oven for 30–35 minutes or until a crust has formed. Allow to cool slightly and then cut into squares.

Chocolate Fridge Cake

This recipe makes a substantial amount, but it will keep and, in fact, gets better in an airtight container. It is more of a chocolate snack than a cake.

Utensils Long plastic container or terrine

450g/1lb digestive biscuits
(about 15)
100g/4oz pecans
100g/4oz pistachio nuts
10 glacé cherries

1 Break the biscuits into small pieces directly into a large bowl. Add the pecans, pistachios and cherries.

150g/5oz butter
1 dessertspoon golden syrup
1 tablespoon sugar
225g/8oz good-quality
chocolate

2 Put the rest of the ingredients into a bowl and put either on a low heat over a pan of simmering water or in a microwave to melt.

3 Mix all the ingredients together and place in the container which simply acts as a mould. To ease the turning out, line the container with cling film first, leaving plenty of extra film at the edges to fold over the top. Leave in the fridge to firm up.

4 When firm, turn out and cut into chunky slices. This cake can be kept in an airtight container and will taste even better after a couple of days (if you can wait that long to eat it!).

chapter ten

girls call
the shots

'Can I fix you a drink?'

And we don't mean crack open a six-pack. How much more cool is it to whip up a cocktail or, even more impressive, to serve up a shot? Not only have we included some classic favourites in this chapter – such as Pina Colada and Sea Breeze – but there are some shots which are guaranteed to get your party started on the right note. The last recipe in this section is for a Bloody Mary – you might be needing it after trying some of the previous ones!

Vodka Espresso

1 large shot of vodka
1 single espresso

Pour into a glass with ice, cover the top and shake well until frothy. Pour into a clean glass to serve. Drink immediately.

Pina Colada

A classic – delicious even if it is considered a little tacky by some!

Equal measures of:
White rum
Crème de cacao
Cream of coconut
Pineapple juice

Mix all ingredients together and serve with or without ice in a tall glass. Add a fancy umbrella!

Cosmopolitan

Apparently this is the absolute favourite of most ladies who frequent the American Bar at London's Savoy Hotel!

20ml/¾fl oz vodka
20ml/¾fl oz Cointreau
40ml/1½fl oz cranberry juice
1½ tablespoons fresh lime juice

Put all the ingredients in a cocktail shaker and shake vigorously. Serve without ice.

Sea Breeze

A classic long drink.

Equal measures of:
Vodka
Grapefruit juice
Cranberry juice

Shake all ingredients together in a cocktail shaker. Serve in a tall glass with ice.

Prevention

Another favourite with the ladies, albeit a 'virgin' cocktail, as recommended by the American Bar at the Savoy Hotel.

Measure the following to make a total of 100ml/3⅓fl oz:
Banana
Passionfruit
Cranberry juice
Orange juice
Apple juice
Grapefruit juice

Put all the ingredients in a blender and blend until smooth. Serve in a goblet with ice.

Lemon Drop Shot

The only shot that Roberta will 'shoot'!

20ml/¾fl oz lemon vodka
20ml/¾fl oz triple sec
20ml/¾fl oz lemon juice

Mix together and serve in a frozen shot glass with a sugared lemon garnish.

Margherita

Always a success.

Equal measures of:
Tequila
Lime juice
Cointreau

Mix all the ingredients together in a shaker and serve with or without ice. The edge of the glass can be dipped in salt if you wish although watch out for a possible side effect – hangover dehydration!

Raspberry Martini

Popular with the hot chicks who frequent London's Met Bar.

A few fresh raspberries
12ml/½fl oz raspberry purée
60ml/2¼fl oz vodka
12.5ml crème de framboise
2 drops orange bitters
1 teaspoon gum syrup or sugar syrup
Frozen raspberry to garnish

'Smash' the fresh raspberries in a cocktail shaker, then add the raspberry purée, vodka, crème de framboise, syrup, orange bitters and some ice. Shake and strain into a martini glass with a frozen raspberry placed in the bottom.

TVR's

½ can Red Bull
1 shot vodka
1 shot tequila

Stir, mix with ice and serve.

Bloody Mary

1 part vodka to 4 parts fresh tomato juice
Fresh horseradish
Good squeeze lemon juice
Worcester sauce
Sprinkling of celery salt
Dash of Tabasco

In a tall glass, mix together the vodka and fresh tomato juice. The rest of the ingredients should be stirred in according to taste. Bear in mind that the celery salt is a very important ingredient. Serve chilled.

chapter eleven
puddings
galore

Not many people can resist a pudding

We've tried to give a good cross-section here so that you have something to suit every occasion and every season. It's not always essential to make a pudding when entertaining, as a few good quality cheeses can be just as satisfying. It has to be said, though, that a home-made pudding always goes down a treat, especially with the men. From this chapter you can try your hand with the simplest Lemon Meringue Ice Cream and work your way up to the more advanced Pear Tatin, both equally delicious.

Nigella Lawson's Calvados Syllabub

Syllabub is one of those ethereal, creamy confections which seem at odds with the description 'pudding'. But this scented, whipped cream, piled up to swell cloudily out of its container, is a perfect way to end dinner and gloriously easy to boot.

Utensils Mixing bowl, whisk, 4 serving glasses

8 tablespoons dry cider
2 tablespoons Calvados
¼ teaspoon ground cinnamon
4 tablespoons caster sugar
Juice of 1 lemon
300ml/10fl oz double cream

1 Put the cider, Calvados, ground cinnamon, sugar and lemon juice in a bowl and stir until the sugar has dissolved. Keep on stirring as you gradually pour in the cream. Then, using a wire whisk or an electric one at low speed, whip the syllabub until it is about to form soft peaks. It should occupy some notional territory between solid and liquid so be careful not to let the cream become too thick or, indeed, to go further and curdle.

4 cinnamon sticks (optional)

2 Spoon the syllabub into the glasses and puncture each semi-solid mound with a cinnamon stick or simply dust the uneven tops with the merest haze of ground cinnamon.

Orange Cookies

These cookies are very easy to make and use only a few store cupboard ingredients. They will happily keep for a while in an airtight container, unless, that is, you eat them before they make it into the container.

Utensils Large baking tray, wire cooling rack

110g/4¼oz butter at room temperature (leave out or microwave for a few seconds to aid the creaming process)
50g/2oz caster sugar
Zest of 1 orange

1 Pre-heat the oven to 190°C/375°C/Gas 5. Beat the butter and sugar together in a bowl until it changes to a lighter, paler texture. Add the orange zest.

150g/5oz self-raising flour

2 Stir in the flour and, when completely blended, take a walnut-size piece and roll into a rough ball. Place on the baking tray leaving a 4cm/1½in gap between each dough ball. Dip a fork in water and use it to gently flatten each ball to roughly 5mm/¼in thick. Bake for 5–10 minutes or until flat and just golden brown.

3 Leave to cool on the tray until the cookies start to firm and then transfer them onto a wire cooling rack. Serve with ice cream or just on their own. They will keep well in an airtight container.

Top Tip Use a zester to peel the orange as it is the easiest way to get to the peel; then chop the tiny strands. Chopping the peel gives it a finer texture, which is imperative for the tiny cookies.

Poached Peaches Cardinal

Serves 4
Preparation and Cooking Time:
40 minutes

Peaches are at their best during the late summer and autumn.

Utensils Large saucepan, food processor, hand blender and plastic sieve

200g/7oz caster sugar
4 ripe peaches

1 Fill the saucepan three-quarters full of water, add the sugar and bring to a simmer to make a syrup. Place the peaches in the sugar syrup and leave to simmer gently for 30 minutes. Leave to cool.

500g/1lb 1½oz fresh or frozen raspberries
Icing sugar to taste, optional

2 Place the raspberries in the food processor or use a container and hand blender. This will make a fine purée very quickly. Pour into a fine plastic sieve and push through to leave a beautiful and glossy sauce. Taste and add a little icing sugar if needed.

3 The peaches are cooked when they feel 'squidgy'. Leave them to cool in the liquid, covered, in the fridge. Once cooked and cooled, they can be peeled easily – if the skin is thick, peel it off; however, if it is thin, leave it on.

4 To serve, place each peach into an individual glass and pour over the sauce. Serve with cream, ice cream or just on their own in their full unadulterated glory!

Nougat Parfait

This takes some time to prepare but is well worth the effort. Once frozen, it can simply be cut and put back in the freezer as required. The quantities here will make quite a large amount.

Utensils Baking tray, hand whisk, mixing bowl, large terrine dish/square loaf tin or ramekins

100g/4oz flaked almonds
70g/2¾oz icing sugar

1 Pre-heat the oven to 200°C/400°F/Gas 6. Place the almonds on a baking tray and mix with the icing sugar. Sprinkle with just enough water to coat the almonds with a thick-ish paste. Put the tray into the oven and bake for 4–5 minutes or until a light golden brown. Remove from the oven and leave to cool.

50g/2oz caster sugar
100g/4oz honey
200ml/7fl oz water
8 egg yolks

2 Put the sugar, honey and water in a small saucepan and leave for about 3 minutes on a high heat to bubble and caramelise slightly and to make a sugar syrup. Whisk the egg yolks in a large mixing bowl to a pale colour and then gradually add the sugar syrup. The heat from the syrup will gradually thicken the yolks. Continue to whisk until coolish.

500ml/17fl oz whipping cream

3 Whisk the cream until it's thick and 'dollopy'.

50ml/2fl oz Grand Marnier
Zest of 1 orange

4 Combine all the ingredients in a large bowl by carefully folding with a spatula, gently breaking the almonds into smaller pieces as you go. Line the tin or mould with cling film, leaving extra over the edges. Pour the mixture in level with the top. Wrap the extra cling film over the sides. Freeze immediately for at least six hours.

200g/8oz apricots
4 tablespoons sugar
Water to cover

5 Put the apricots, sugar and water into a pan, cover and simmer for 15–20 minutes until the apricots are soft. Purée in a food processor adding a little water to make a pouring consistency.

6 Serve a slice on individual plates with a good dollop of sauce. When frozen, the parfait will be easily removed from the tin with a good tug of the cling film.

Top Tip Use a sharp knife dipped in boiling water to cut the parfait. You could also use ramekins instead of a terrine tin.

Tina's Cheesecake

This is the ultimate cheesecake and was created by Roberta's mother, Tina. It is velvety smooth yet light and rich – it's also guaranteed not to last long. You can finely shave some good quality chocolate over the top if you want although, quite honestly, it is just divine on its own.

Utensils Food processor (optional) or rolling pin, 25cm/10in springform baking tin, electric hand blender, small saucepan, mixing bowl

200g/7oz digestive biscuits
125g/4½oz unsalted butter, melted
Butter for greasing

1 Pre-heat the oven to 150°C/300°F/Gas 2. Process the biscuits in the blender until they are like crumbs, or crush them in a plastic bag using a rolling pin. Melt the butter in a saucepan and add the biscuit crumbs. Grease the bottom of a springform tin with butter and press in the biscuit crumbs with the back of a spoon to form a base.

600g/1lb 5oz cream cheese
3 large eggs
3 teaspoons vanilla essence
150g/5oz caster sugar
3 dessertspoons lemon juice, freshly squeezed

2 Using a hand whisk or blender, in a bowl mix together the cream cheese and add eggs one at a time. Add the vanilla essence, caster sugar and lemon, and fold in briefly. Pour over the biscuit base and bake in the middle of the oven for 25 minutes; then remove and stand until cool (approximately 1 hour). Turn the oven up to 190°C/375°F/Gas 5.

600ml/20fl oz sour cream
1 teaspoon vanilla extract
1 dessertspoon caster sugar

3 In the mixing bowl, beat together the sour cream, vanilla essence and caster sugar with a wooden spoon to make the topping. When the cheese mixture is cold, pour on the sour cream topping and cook for 5 minutes in the middle of the very hot oven. Remove from the oven and leave to cool. Once the cheesecake is cold, place it in the fridge to set for a few hours or preferably overnight.

Old-fashioned Apple Pie

This traditional dessert cannot be topped. Great for an autumnal Sunday lunch as apples are best during September and October. You can also team them up with their perfect partner – blackberries – during October.

Utensils Pie dish

175g/6oz plain flour
40g/1½oz lard
40g/1½oz butter

1 To make the pastry, put the flour and fats into a food processor and pulse until well blended. Add a couple of spoonfuls of cold water and pulse again. The pastry should easily come together in a ball and feel quite moist. Turn out onto a flat work surface and knead into a ball. Leave to rest while preparing the apples.

700g/1lb 9oz apples (Bramleys or Granny Smiths)
75g/3oz caster sugar
½ teaspoon ground cinnamon

2 Peel the apples, quarter and remove the cores. Chop into large 2–3cm/¾–1¼in chunks, pile into the pie dish and mix with the sugar and cinnamon.

A little extra flour for dusting
1 egg, beaten

3 Preheat the oven to 200°C/400°F/Gas 6. Dust the work surface with a little flour and roll out the pastry into a large round to fit over the top of the pie dish. Keep the pastry moving in between each 'roll' as this prevents it from sticking. Lay the pastry over the apples and cut away any overlapping edges using a sharp knife. Decorate the top if you wish, then brush the top with beaten egg. Cut a small slit in the middle of the pastry to release the steam. Bake in the top of the oven for about 35 minutes or until the pastry is golden brown.

4 Serve hot with ice cream or double cream.

Serves 6-8

Preparation and Cooking Time:
1 hour

Chocolate Tart

This tart may take a little more time than the average pudding but if you cook it in the morning for the evening, you won't have to do anything to it until you're ready to eat. It is definitely worth the extra effort and the taste is totally different from a shop-bought version. The chocolate mixture is only cooked for a few minutes, which keeps it gooey in the middle.

Utensils 24cm/9½in loose bottomed tart tin, electric hand whisk, food processor, saucepan and bowl to fit without touching the bottom (for melting the chocolate)

180g/6¼oz plain flour
Pinch of salt
90g/3½oz very cold butter
1 egg yolk mixed with 2 tablespoons cold water
6 tablespoons icing sugar
Extra flour, for dusting

1 Put the flour, salt and butter in the food processor and pulse until it resembles fine breadcrumbs. If you don't have a processor, put the ingredients into a bowl and rub with your fingers. Add the water and egg yolk and mix well or pulse again. Turn out onto a flat work surface and knead gently together. Dust the surface with a little flour and roll into a thin circle, moving after every couple of rolls so the pastry does not stick to the surface. Roll the pastry onto the rolling pin to lift over the tin, 'unravel' and gently push into the base and edges of the tin. Any excess pastry can be rolled over the edge to leave a neat finish. Leave the tin in the fridge or freezer for as long as you can or at least 30 minutes to let the pastry rest.

2 When ready, pre-heat the oven to 190°C/375°F/Gas 5 and put a baking sheet in the middle. Bake the tart base for 20 minutes. If it has been chilled for long enough it will not puff up. However, if it does, simply pierce it with a sharp knife. Keep an eye on it as it should become only a light brown.

3 medium egg yolks
2 medium eggs
3 tablespoons caster sugar

3 Meanwhile prepare the filling. Whisk the yolks, whole eggs and sugar until very thick and pale. If you don't have an electric whisk, do this over a pan of simmering water.

150g/5oz butter
200g/7oz good-quality chocolate, 65% cocoa solids

4 Melt the butter with the chocolate on a low heat, either in a microwave or over a pan of simmering water. Pour onto the egg mixture while still warm, fold carefully and pour into the tart tin. Pop into the oven on top of the still hot baking sheet for 8 minutes.

Cocoa, for dusting

5 Remove and leave to cool completely, then dust the top with cocoa before cutting. Serve with lots of berries and a dollop of crème fraîche.

Mont Blanc

Chestnuts only seem to make an appearance in this country at Christmas. This recipe, however, makes use of the particularly delicious tinned and puréed variety. If you can't get the sweetened version, just add a little sugar.

Utensils Large baking tray, baking parchment, large bowl, electric whisk

6 medium egg whites
350g/12oz caster sugar

1 Preheat the oven to 180°C/350°F/Gas 4. Line the baking tray with baking parchment. Whisk the egg whites in a large bowl until white and quite firm. Then whisk in the sugar 1 tablespoonful at a time, until the meringue becomes very thick and glossy.

2 teaspoons cornflour
1 teaspoon vinegar

2 Mix together the cornflour and vinegar, then mix into the meringue. Spoon onto the paper and shape into a large round with a dipped centre. Bake for 5 minutes to crisp up the outside, then turn down the heat to 140°C/275°F/Gas 1 and bake for a further 1¼ hours. Leave to cool on the paper, then carefully peel away and transfer to a large serving dish.

2x 250g/9oz tins crème de marron (sweetened chestnut purée)
A little icing sugar
250ml/8fl oz crème fraîche

3 Mix the chestnut purée with the icing sugar and spread over the now cooled meringue. Top with the crème fraîche.

4 Serve reasonably quickly, as it will not stand for too long.

Poached Plums with Red Wine

Serves 4
Preparation and Cooking Time:
20 minutes

Plums are best during September. This simple recipe can be prepared in advance and makes a great, healthy autumnal desert.

Utensils 1 large saucepan

700g/1lb 9oz ripe plums

1 Cut the plums in half and remove the stones. Halve the plums again and place in the saucepan.

200g/7oz sugar
1 glass red wine

2 Just cover the plums with water, add the sugar and wine. Bring to the boil and turn down to a simmer for 5–10 minutes or until the plums are just soft.

3 tablespoons mascarpone
3 tablespoons fromage frais
A little sugar to taste

3 Serve warm or cold in tall glasses with mascarpone and fromage frais mixed with a little sugar.

Lemon Curd Pavlova

Serves 4
Preparation and Cooking Time:
1 hour 20 minutes

Utensils Large baking tray, baking parchment, large bowl, electric whisk

6 medium egg whites
350g/12oz caster sugar

1 Preheat the oven to 180°C/350°F/Gas 4. Line the baking tray with baking parchment. Whisk the egg whites in a large bowl until white and quite firm, then whisk in the sugar 1 tablespoonful at a time, until the meringue becomes very thick and glossy.

2 teaspoons cornflour
1 teaspoon vinegar

2 Mix together the cornflour and vinegar, then mix into the meringue. Spoon onto the paper and shape into a large round with a dipped centre. Bake for 5 minutes to crisp up the outside, then turn down the heat to 140°C/275°F/Gas 1 and bake for a further 1¼ hours.

250ml/8fl oz double cream
125g/4½oz good-quality lemon curd

3 Leave to cool on the paper, then carefully peel away and transfer to a large serving dish. If it does break don't worry as the cream will cover it up. Whip the cream until just thick then spread it over the meringue top. Then pile the lemon curd in the middle.

1 pomegranate

4 Sprinkle the pomegranate seeds over the top to decorate. This will sit for a while but not too long.

Lemon Meringue Ice Cream

Serves 4

Preparation and Cooking Time:
10 minutes, plus 1 hour freezing

This is a very simple pudding for when you really can't be bothered to have a full-on cooking session. For some reason the meringue does not freeze and the lemon curd adds a sharp contrast.

Utensils Large mixing bowl, plastic container

500ml/17fl oz good-quality vanilla ice cream
6 heaped dessertspoons good-quality lemon curd
2 ready-made meringue nests

1   Scrape the vanilla ice cream into a large mixing bowl – it should be slightly soft. Spoon in the lemon curd. Break the meringue into large chunks and add to the bowl. Mix together carefully but don't overdo it – the resulting effect should be rippled.

2   Place into a container and cover well with cling film or a lid. Place back in the freezer as soon as you can so it does not melt too much. Re-freeze for at least an hour.

3   Serve the ice cream scooped into a large glass dish with a few berries.

Pan-cooked Cherries

Serves 4

Preparation and Cooking Time:
20 minutes

This pudding can only be made in the summer months, when cherries are at their best and cheapest. Try Morello cherries.

Utensils Large frying pan, pitter

2kg/4½lb fresh cherries

2 tablespoons caster sugar
Large glug Kirsch

1   Stone the cherries (if you don't have a pitter, just use your fingers).

2   Place the sugar and Kirsch in a hot pan on a medium heat; stir and add the cherries. Leave on a medium heat until the cherries have cooked a little and some of the juices have been released.

3   Serve in large glasses while hot, with vanilla ice cream.

Pear Tatin

Utensils Tart tatin dish or frying pan 25cm/10in wide

5 pears, semi-ripe

1 Peel the pears, cut in half lengthways and remove the core with a sharp knife.

150g/5oz caster sugar
50g/2oz butter

2 Place the frying pan or tatin dish directly over a medium heat and melt the sugar. Try not to stir too much as it may cause the sugar to grain. Be patient and wait for the sugar to melt and caramelise – it may start in patches which can then be stirred to even out the colour. Don't let the caramel become too dark and burn. Once it is just dark enough (a good caramel colour), stir in the butter a little at a time. Place the pears on top, cut-side upwards – this should be a tight fit – and leave on a medium-low heat for 5 minutes to begin to cook.

A little flour for rolling
275g/10oz packet ready-rolled all-butter puff pastry

3 Pre-heat the oven 200°C/400°F/Gas 6. Dust a flat work surface with flour and roll out the pastry to measure slightly larger than a dinner plate. Use a plate as a template and cut the pastry into a circle.

4 Leave the pears to cool very slightly, then cover with the pastry, ensuring that the edges are tucked down in between the edge of the pan and the pears. Place in the hot oven and leave for 20 minutes.

5 When cooked, leave to rest for a couple of minutes then place a large plate over the top of the pan. Use two cloths to turn out onto a large plate, pears on top. Serve warm with vanilla ice cream or crème fraîche.

Top Tip Tatin tins are quite difficult to find but a good frying pan with a metal handle will suffice.

If the sugar is left too long the tart will not turn out, so put it back in the oven for a couple of minutes and the sugar will soon melt.

INDEX

MAIL ORDER INGREDIENTS

Simply Sausages
– 020 7394 7776

The Spice Shop
– 020 7221 4448
www.thespiceshop.co.uk

The Chocolate Society
– 01423 322230
e-mail: info@chocolate.co.uk
website: www.chocolate.co.uk

Cool Chilli Company
– 0870 902 1145

ABOUT THE AUTHORS

Roberta Moore has worked in public relations and event management for the last ten years, including the sports promotions company of her late father, Bobby Moore. Roberta had her own company in New York City where projects included events for President Clinton and members of the Kennedy family.

Louise Holland's career as a chef has taken her from the Dorchester and Mosimann's to in-house chef at the cookery book mecca, *Books for Cooks*. It was there that she was discovered by the producer of Channel 4's *Light Lunch* show where her culinary expertise took her on to become food producer of *Late Lunch*.

Larder Lads
Louise Holland and Roberta Moore
0 09187081 X
£12.99

To order copies direct from Ebury call TBS Direct credit-card hotline on 012062 55800.

Ebury books are also available from all good booksellers.

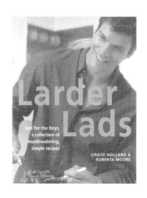